RESTORING IOWA'S DEMOCRACY:

A Citizen's Guide for Improving Iowa's Government and Economic Future.

by

Mark Edelman

**MID-PRAIRIE BOOKS
PARKERSBURG, IOWA
1993**

© Copyright 1993 Mid-Prairie Books

All rights reserved. No part of this book may be used or reproduced in any manner whatsoever without written permission of the publisher.

Printed in the United States of America.

Book composition by Ireland Design & Publishing, Cedar Falls, IA

Cover Photos by Chuck Greiner.

Cover Design by Lonna Nachtigal.

Published by:
Mid-Prairie Books
801 4th Avenue
Parkersburg, IA 50665
319-346-2048

ISBN 0-931209-52-8

RESTORING IOWA'S DEMOCRACY:

A Citizen's Guide for Improving Iowa's Government and Economic Future.

TABLE OF CONTENTS

PREFACE	iv
CHAPTER 1. Rebuilding Iowa's Jobs Base	1
CHAPTER 2. Restoring Fiscal Responsibility	24
CHAPTER 3. Restoring Political Leadership	50
CHAPTER 4. Reinventing Local Government	69
CHAPTER 5. Solving the Health Care Problem	91
CHAPTER 6. Keeping Iowa Number 1 in Education	114
CHAPTER 7. Iowans at the Crossroads	133
SELECTED REFERENCES	138

PREFACE

"Believe in What You Do... Do What You Believe In."
1993 Rotary International Theme.

In Dedication to Nancy, Adam, Alexandria, and Aaron.

Over the past several years, I made a commitment to study Iowa's priority issues and to increase citizen understanding and involvement in the choices we face. Others have participated in that commitment. We experimented with statewide satellite and broadcast TV town meetings, focus groups, and citizen juries before they became popular in the last Presidential campaign. We know their value and we also know the value of local discussion. This book represents a new approach for increasing citizen awareness and participation on Iowa's issues. The approach is designed to honestly assess Iowa's recent history and to raise issues and choices that will determine our future.

In addition to my efforts, this book represents the ideas of many people. Several ideas came from prominent Republicans. Several ideas came from prominent Democrats. Some ideas came from people belonging to United We Stand, Ross Perot's new organization. Other ideas came from just plain folks who participated in our statewide town meetings and focus groups. To all who gave ideas, I offer my thanks. If the ideas look familiar, it is because they came from practical minded Iowans like yourself who are concerned about Iowa.

I particularly want to extend thanks to Jeff Anderson, Ann Campbell, Richard Clem, Lloyd Courter, Paul Coates, Brian Cunningham, Burt Day, Jayne Hager Dee, Dave Dickson, Nancy Edelman, Beth Erickson, Dr. Barry Flinchbaugh, Guy Ghan, Dr. Neil Harl, Becky Johnson, Richard Johnson, Phyllis Ketcham, Eleanor Kniker, Diane Kolmer, Lee Kolmer, Ruth Kaduce, Jeff Kooistra, Hugh LaMont, Roger Linn, Phil Meier, Brian Menz, Sue Mullins, Robert Neymeyer, Art Neu, Dr. Dan Otto, Randy Schmitz, Bill Sherman, Bill Silag, David Swenson, Don Riemenschneider, Rick Ross and four anonymous reviewers. These citizens deserve thanks for their integrity, friendship and time in allowing me to test various ideas and for assisting me in bringing this book to closure. At the same time, I am fully responsible for that which has been written. The views presented are my own and do not represent the official positions of Iowa State University. If there are any perceived short-comings or inadequacies, they are my sole responsibility.

At this time in Iowa's history, rather than limit citizen involvement, information and public discussion in the making of public policy, we need to expand and strengthen citizen participation. We have too much government for the people and need more "Jeffersonian style" government of the people and by the people. There is no challenge more important in assuring the future viability and vitality of our state.

I was initially stimulated to write this book after reading *United We Stand*, the book by Ross Perot. The reason is simple. In many respects, the recent political environment in Iowa has been all too similar to Washington. Gridlock, fiscal irresponsibility, and ethics problems are not unique characteristics of the professional politicians in Washington.

Perhaps Iowa's professional politicians need to be jolted with citizen leaders from across the state who lead by example, who take charge of our state's problems, who lay the cards on the table, who tell the people the facts and the truth, who engage Iowa citizens in the decision-making process, and who listen and work with the people to resolve the issues we face.

We are all in the same boat called the "good ship Iowa." If we the people better understand the nature of the problems we face, then we can put our collective heads together and come up with a practical plan for solving each issue, one at a time.

As a political economist, my job is to analyze behavior in response to political and economic incentives created by public policy and to assist citizens in understanding and improving our political system and economy. No set of public issues are more important than the fundamental rules of our democratic system, our budget, our economy, our local government, our health care and our education. These are the issues covered in this book.

This book is a collection of principles, ideas and positive proposals for the future. However, to improve our future performance, we must also understand and evaluate the events of the past decade. In writing this book, I did not want to violate principles of professional ethics by "impugning anyone's personal motives." Each person in public situations is entitled to his or her own motives and should not be attacked on that basis alone.

What each did or didn't do in discharging public responsibilities is more important than motives. However, motives are often needed to understand the actions taken. Thus, motives are only discussed when there is corroborating evidence. References to individuals have been dropped in favor of references to offices, institutions, or interest groups.

To keep democracy strong, citizens are entitled to evaluate and judge the behavior and performance of public officials and democratic institutions. If someone thinks we are not doing things in a proper fashion, they dig up evidence that helps to explain the present behavior and why we are supposedly doing the wrong things. That is the nature of public officials and public institutions. We are fair game.

A similar process is used in this book. Statistics and circumstantial evidence are used to evaluate recent events, the state's future agenda, and the performance of those who played a role and may play a role in the future. A case is made for changing Iowa's agenda. It matters not to me whether existing leaders take up this charge or whether new citizen leaders emerge to direct Iowa's course.

In deciding whether some events should be included, the Rotary Four-Way Test was used: "Is it the truth? Is it fair to all concerned? Will it build good will and better friendships? Will it be beneficial to all concerned?" Clearly some people may conclude I violated the tests. However, being beneficial to all and building good will does not occur when an elite group dominates the democratic process to further its own special interests. In contrast, good will and trust are earned over the long run, when democratic institutions use principles of equal representation, tolerance for the views of others, and statesmanship in protecting the interests of all citizens.

Chapter 1. Rebuilding Iowa's Jobs Base.

1. Heed The Current Warning Signs.

Citizens in Iowa and the Midwest are working longer hours and receiving less. Often both parents must work to make ends meet. Many new families are having trouble buying their first home. Young people coming out of our high schools and colleges are having a difficult time finding jobs in Iowa. Many of Iowa's rural communities continue to lose population at a rapid rate.

All one has to do to gain a sense of Iowa's eroding economic base over the past decade is to review the media list for a recent six month period of plant closings and jobs lost: White-New Idea was to lay off more than 400 workers in Charles City at a tractor transmission plant scheduled to close by mid-1993. While Marshalltown was spared the loss of 600 jobs by Lennox, Fisher Controls of Marshalltown placed 190 workers on indefinite lay off in December 1992. Northwestern Railroad relocated 200 customer service positions from Boone to Chicago. General Motors Corporation announced it would lay off 200 workers in Sioux City at a plant that will close in 1993. U.S. West Communications announced a lay off of 150 Iowa workers in early 1993. Crystal Tips manufacturing in Spirit Lake moved 150 jobs to Texas. Chamberlain Manufacturing in Waterloo announced plans to lay off 90 workers or half of its workforce in 1993. Jimmy Dean in Osceola announced a plant closing with a potential loss of 150 workers. The distribution of layoffs and plant closing announcements were all over Iowa.

Where does the Iowa Department of Employment Services project the greatest increase in Iowa jobs for 1993 to 2000? The list includes: cashiers and retail clerks, janitors and cleaners, general managers and executives, truck drivers, secretaries, bookkeepers and office assistants, registered nurses, nurses aides and orderlies, sales representatives, food preparers and cooks. The only ones on the list that produce a product are the cooks.

We are replacing manufacturing jobs that pay $10 per hour with service sector jobs that pay $8 per hour. For

1992, total Iowa jobs were up by one percent but the number of manufacturing jobs declined again. A story repeated in the past decade.

Politicians and economists rationalize the trends as a part of something bigger than Iowa. They say it is a result of national restructuring within the manufacturing sectors. While this is true, one must wonder if our successes would also be attributed to outside influences as well. It is precisely this attitude that lulls the average citizen into believing we are powerless in redirecting our own resources toward achieving something better.

We have become too comfortable with leaving our problems to other people who supposedly know more about how to solve them. Leave our health insurance to the health experts. Leave our education to the education experts. Leave our government budgets to the professional politicians. For a decade, we have left our problems to the professionals and it has not worked.

Citizens are frustrated. Instead of sustainable economic development, we see race tracks and river boats. We see deficits, creative accounting, and ethics problems. Do Iowans have the courage to ask if there is a better plan or a better way? Would the results be different if Iowa had a more progressive economic policy? I believe the answer is "yes."

It is simple 8th grade math. If we want Iowa's standard of living to increase, we must add the jobs with above average wages for the community. Sure, every community has a different wage scale. A wage that does not look good to one community might look pretty good in another. But the economic principle is that each community must focus on jobs that pay above the prevailing local average wage so the community can prosper in the long run.

If you add jobs with below average wages, the average standard of living declines unless everyone works longer and harder. Replacing higher wage manufacturing jobs with lower wage service sector jobs may slow the eroding jobs base temporarily, but it will also lower Iowa's standard of living in the long run.

In spite of efforts to attract new businesses, Iowa's investing environment is not significantly different from the average investing environment of other states. Contrary to what many citizens might think, Iowa has historically judged its tax and investing policies based on whether Iowa ranked above or below 25th among the 50 states. The simple straight forward conclusion is that average tax policies coupled with mature industries and eroding economic trends is a sure fire formula for continued erosion of the high-paying jobs.

Each year, Iowans are told we only need a few more years before investments in new high-tech endeavors begin to pay off. Yes, we have had some initial successes. However, the bottom line is the status quo has simply not been enough to turn around or prevent Iowa's jobs base and economy from long-term erosion.

At the same time, not all the news is bad news. In 1992, for the first time in several years, Iowa's six percent growth in personal income per capita was greater than surrounding states. This was due in part to Iowa's bumper corn crop last year. However, the longer term reality has been that Iowa's jobs base and Iowa's economy has been growing more slowly for the past decade than that of the neighboring states. And this year, flood damage will likely dampen Iowa's economic growth rate.

As a result, national groups like the Corporation for Enterprise Development give Iowa a mixed report card: "A" for last year's economic performance, "D" for business vitality and "C" for future growth. The 1993 grades are based on about 50 indicators. While Iowa ranks high in terms of high school graduation, employment, and adult literacy, our job market doesn't keep our graduates in Iowa. Iowa ranks in the lower third in terms of college attainment among the adult workforce and proportion of scientists and engineers in the workforce. Iowa ranks in the lower third in terms of several measures of business investment, growth in trade with other states, and creation of new companies.

We have reached a time in Iowa's history that we cannot afford the slow growth status quo. Increasingly, many Iowa citizens are wondering whether the time has come for common sense and progressive management to change the basic rules of the game to see if we can achieve something better.

2. Longer Term Danger Signals Ahead.

What will be the consequences of the status quo trends 30 years from now? In 1990, Iowa ranked third among the 50 states in the proportion of its citizens over age 65 and first in citizens over age 85. While it is nice to possess longevity and retention of senior citizens, this trend also represents the outmigration of young people from rural communities, outmigration of young people from Iowa, and outmigration of jobs and income opportunities. This generational imbalance means relationships between the public and private sectors will become increasingly volatile, particularly in Iowa's rural communities.

At the present time, there are three Iowans of working age for every two Iowans that are retired or in school. If present demographic trends continue for 30 years, there will be only one Iowan of working age for every Iowan who is retired or in school. There simply won't be enough people in the work force to continue present levels of real support, unless something dramatic occurs.

On one hand, if we protect our competitiveness and limit growth in revenue collections, we may be forced to make major cuts in education, health care, and other public services. On the other hand, if we attempt to meet growing education and health care demands, tax increases will overwhelm our state's income generating capacity and erode our international competitiveness.

You say you don't like the options. But, there are only so many ways out of the box. Is there a third approach? The answer is "yes." The third approach is to dramatically increase Iowa's economic pie, income generating capacity and high paying jobs.

Instead of accepting the first two status quo options, what if we examined the third option? What would it take to dramatically increase Iowa's economic pie to be competitive with the Japanese and Germans? What shape would such a plan take? What would we have to do? What would the results be? How could it be done and what are the principles to be followed? Let's answer the questions in reverse order. First, the principles of the plan.

3. We Are All in the Same Boat.

In spite of the doom and gloom, most rural communities have experienced some successful economic development efforts. It is wrong to think that only the counties with growing populations have been successful in their economic development efforts. There have been rural community successes all over the state. The only problem is that successes in many rural communities have been overshadowed by plant closings, population declines and eroding economic indicators reported by the media.

Without the rural successes, Iowa would be much worse off. In fact, the rural successes are just as important, if not more important, than urban successes if we are concerned about the state's total collective bottom line. The present urban growth will continue to provide a strong engine for future economic development in urban counties of the state. However, if Iowa's rural infrastructure is utilized at a lower and lower percent of total capacity, the whole state will pay the bill and Iowa will be limited in her ability to progress economically.

Urban Iowa cannot fence itself off from the half of the population that lives in the 86 rural counties of the state. If nothing else, half of the voters live in rural counties. Again, we are all in the same boat, rural-urban divisions will only slow our overall progress and growth in Iowa's economy.

Unless we change the status quo by building new bridges between rural and urban Iowa interests in policymaking, our children will watch their income generating capacity and competitiveness erode or they will face major cuts in education, health care and other services. Instead of the status quo, Iowa's political leadership must insist on rural-urban coalitions as a matter of course. No bill should be signed into law unless it is a win-win proposition for both rural and urban Iowa.

There is an old adage, "if more people are rocking the boat, less people are rowing and progress forward is slowed." Under status quo leadership, Iowans have become more divided. We have divisions between the government administration and state employees. We have divisions between the private and the public sector. We have divisions between rural and urban communities. We have divisions between corporate elite and small business. Too many are rocking the boat instead of rowing together.

The simple fact is that for Iowa to achieve the maximum rate of economic growth, we must all be inspired to do our best. Rapid progress requires important contributions from both the public and private sector. Both must be well-managed, efficient, and productive. Both rural and urban Iowa citizens must have the opportunity to contribute and receive benefits from Iowa's economic development. If we are to work efficiently and productively together to achieve our collective potential, small business, individual citizens, as well as corporate giants, must have opportunity and access to critical resources. We are all in the same boat together. If we cannot work together better in the future, Iowa's economic progress will continue to erode.

4. Plug the Leaks; Retain More Dollars in Iowa.

Before we can begin to think about repositioning Iowa's economy for the long-term, we must plug the present leaks. Plugging the leaks means changing government policy and private behavior to maximize the dollars retained in Iowa's economy.

This is the same principle that many farmers and business people use when they visit their tax accountant in December. Their goal is to maximize the amount of income they can legally retain by minimizing next year's income taxes. The accountant recommends a specific tax avoidance strategy that is perfectly legal. If the farmer or business person has faith in their tax accountant they may even follow the strategy without fully understanding the details of the tax law or how it works.

Similarly, we need to do the same thing to state tax policy. Most Iowans don't care how complex the tax policy strategy is. They are interested in the "bottom line." They are interested if the policy means they have more total income left at the end of the year because they each paid $50 less total taxes.

Plugging the leaks in Iowa's private sector economy could mean providing incentives to replace out-of-state suppliers of raw materials with in-state suppliers whenever possible. More total dollars would be retained in Iowa's economy as a result.

Plugging the leaks in the public sector could mean adjusting state tax policy to conserve dollars retained in Iowa. For example, state government spends more than $40 million on farmland property tax credits per year to reduce the local property taxes paid by all owners of Iowa farmland. A large share of these credits go to absentee owners living out of state.

If the intent of lawmakers is to assist young and beginning farmers, then the property tax credits could be redesigned into young and beginning farmer credits that retain more dollars in Iowa. If the intent of the lawmakers is to assist farm operators, then the property tax credits could be redesigned into farm operator credits that retain more dollars in Iowa.

If the policymaker intent is to stimulate agricultural investment in Iowa, the property tax credits could be redesigned into agricultural investment credits. Under these credits, only those who invested in Iowa qualify for receiving the property tax credit. Again more state spending would be retained in Iowa.

Another example of plugging the leaks is to shift Iowa's tax policy from taxes that are not federally deductible to those that are. One way to accomplish this would be to replace Iowa's sales tax, which is not federally deductible, with an equal increase in state income tax that is deductible. An analysis of this idea suggests Iowans could collectively save up to $200 million in total federal, state, and local taxes each year. This amounts to an extra $150 to $200 per family per year.

Other ideas have come from numerous consultant studies done by the Legislature. For example, a major tax study was recently completed and most of the ideas are still sitting on the shelf. What really perplexes citizens is that some politicians jump at the opportunity to land a $20 million business in the state. Yet, there seems to be little interest in activities that would add $200 million to Iowa's economy by leaving a little bit more in every citizen's pocket-book at the end of the year.

Citizens hope there would be less interest in cutting ribbons and getting political credit than in doing the homework to be innovative. But several recent events provide reasons to be skeptical. Yes, new ideas may be risky. Sure, we may need adjustments. But that is what pilot projects are for. That's how you make new innovations work. The sad fact is no one will ever know whether citizens would like some proposals unless a pilot test is tried in a few counties.

5. Increase Citizen Saving and Investment in Iowa.

Iowa citizens are the owners of Iowa. We all have a stake in the future of our state. From the richest Iowan to the poorest, we all should be given the opportunity and incentives to save, invest, and invent our state's future. We all should reap returns in relation to our investments.

Most companies invest a minimum of 10 to 20 percent of the annual earnings in product research and market development. Other firms focusing on growth invest as much as 80 percent. As a nation, we are saving at a rate of 4 percent of our income compared to the Japanese at 18 percent and Germans at 10 percent.

As a percent of Gross Domestic Product (GDP), private industry funded research and development is 1.5 times greater in Germany and 2 times greater in Japan compared to the U.S. As a percent of GDP, gross plant and equipment spending is 1.5 time greater in Germany and 2 times greater in Japan than in the U.S.

In a democracy, maximum economic growth can only be attained if the people have incentives, culture, and mindset to reinvest in their own economic future. With interest rates at record low levels, we must focus on other incentives to increase saving and investment in Iowa. Instead of a narrow set of incentives that provides favors for a few elite special interests, we need broad incentives that generate citizen participation, ownership, and public support in the process.

What if Iowans saved and reinvested 10 to 20 percent of our annual income instead of four percent? The difference would be an additional $3 to $6 billion of annual investment in Iowa. If the average new plant costs $100 million, you could build 30 to 60 new plants in Iowa each year. Can you imagine how many companies Iowa citizens could create with $3 to $6 billion?

Four percent of income means the average family savings is about $1,200 per year. If we increase it to 10 to 20 percent, the average family savings and reinvestment would be $3,000 to $6,000 per year. Sure, in the short run this is probably unrealistic. But, our international competition is doing it!

Let's be more practical. What if we could come up with an additional $500 million per year? That would only be an extra $500 per family. That is a lot for many people but not much for others. Think of the strategic companies Iowans could create, expand, or buy and relocate to Iowa with $500 million per year.

Now Iowans aren't interested in raising taxes because we have just had the largest tax increase in Iowa history. So the question is, can we create incentives for saving and investing without raising total tax collections? Yes, we can. We simply shift the incentives in the present Iowa tax code. We can eliminate many of Iowa's present tax subsidies to create a new and different set of tax breaks that would reward all Iowans, rich and poor, for saving and investing in Iowa's future.

Capitalism cannot operate without capital. Our economic engine needs capital, if we are serious about reversing the erosion in our jobs base. If we reinvest in Iowa's future, yes, consumption may be slowed in the short run. But, it will be higher in the long run as a result of the future economic growth and income generated from higher levels of investment. In order to reap a higher return tomorrow, one must invest today. The simple principle is true for family, community, state, or nation.

What are the steps? First, citizens are not going to increase savings at low interest rates without a change in tax policy incentives. Iowa can create a pro-savings tax policy and a savings ethic like we used to have a few decades ago. Several good ideas include expanded use of tax free retirement accounts, tax free college tuition funds, tax free medical savings accounts, tax free home equity pools, and other tax free savings accounts.

Second, we must tie the changes in our tax policy on savings to the act of investing in Iowa. This creates a tax code that is pro-investment. It is not good enough to encourage citizens to save if the savings are invested outside of Iowa. The present tax policy and regulatory incentives encourage home town financial institutions to invest in government securities. Regulators have penalized local lenders for making risky investments in their local communities.

This must be changed so that Iowa is viewed to be different. We can change Iowa policy so that our state is viewed to be different from the other 49 states in regards to our savings and investment policy. We must strive to be among the top ten states in terms of savings and investment indicators if we want to make a difference.

Third, our policy should foster employee-owned, patron-owned, and Iowa citizen-owned businesses where possible. Let me relate a story of a remote community in the Dakotas located more than 150 miles from an interstate. Community leaders decided not to waste money on advertising because they would never be able to convince an outside company board of directors to invest in their local community. So, they pooled their money, flew to the Southwest, and bought a company. Then they relocated the plant to the local community.

If local citizens are not willing to invest in their own community, there is not much hope in convincing outsiders to invest in it either. Recently, business people in Ames tried a similar strategy with a developing corporate jet manufacturer called VisionAire Corporation. Several local business people bought into the company. When members of the board of directors live in a single local community, the company is more likely to locate a plant there and it is less likely to pick up and leave. As a result, public policy should give incentives to encourage employee-owned, patron-owned, and Iowa citizen-owned businesses.

Fourth, we need a new kind of investment instrument or tool to make it easier for Iowans to receive competitive returns while safely investing in local industries, local communities, and jobs within the state. The corporate jet manufacturing plant with 350 jobs would have helped to diversify Iowa's economy and seemed to be synergistic with the goals of building on the engineering and technology expertise in Iowa. However, the deal-breaking constraint was a lack of risk capital. Investors needed $5.5 million to develop the concept and designate that the plant would be located in Ames. Only $900,000 had been pledged when the date passed. The approach was good but there was a lack of investment capital and perhaps too much risk.

Presently, it is easy for Iowans to invest their savings in national money markets using payroll deductions for a variety of savings and investment instruments. However, which funds do you invest in if you want to invest in Iowa's future jobs base? All Iowans should have the same incentives to invest in Iowa's future jobs and economic base as they do in payroll deductions for investing in their children's education or their retirement.

We need Iowa's financial industry and government to work together to create a system of tax free Iowa Development Funds. When Iowans make payroll deduction investments, they would know Iowa Development Funds are invested in their community, region, or state to create Iowa's future jobs. The funds could be locally or regionally controlled by community leaders and recognized financial experts instead of controlled by state politicians. This would help to assure that benefits from research and development are distributed to all Iowa communities and citizens.

Finally, we must unlock the savings that are locked up in long-term assets. As an example, urban developers in Iowa often cannot access new land for development from farmers unless they buy additional farmland in rural areas for trade. The farmers near the urban growth centers are unwilling to sell due to the capital gains tax, but they can avoid the tax with a trade.

Presently, citizens in Iowa and most other states have little incentive to sell long-term assets. A citizen who bought property for $10,000 in 1983 immediately pays about $3,000 in taxes if he or she sells it for $21,000 in 1993, even though there has only been a $1,000 real income gain after you adjust for $10,000 in inflation. Therefore, the capital gains tax is greater than the real income gain from holding the asset. So, a person who sells the long term asset not only loses the real income gain, but also is made 15 percent worse off than a person who does not sell the asset.

From an economic perspective, if we only want to tax the real income gain from the sale of the asset, we should deduct the inflation from the capital gain before we tax it. This is called indexing capital gains to inflation. Under our present system, the Iowa and U.S. tax policy levels a huge tax penalty—due to inflation—on those who sell long-term assets. Changing Iowa's tax policy in these areas would gain national attention and would demonstrate that our business and investing environment is more than talk and better than other states.

We need to create a state of entrepreneurs. The three biggest government policy factors eroding our international competitiveness are taxes to pay the interest on our national debt, the cost of our health care policies, and our treatment of our capital gains. No other major industrialized nation except the U.S. taxes long-term capital gains in the same manner as ordinary income. And we wonder why our business leaders focus on short run profits instead of long-term investments that would improve productivity and competitiveness.

Regardless of whether we like it or not, we will not likely see dramatic increases in the long-term investment required to improve productivity and competitiveness until we provide greater rewards to those who take long-term risks. Even if national policy is changed, that means Iowans must examine how we can make our capital investment policies more favorable than other states.

These tax policy changes should not be used as a way of lowering taxes for the wealthy, middle class, or poor. Limitations may be appropriate so the capital gains are not all spent on vacations to Florida and to assure citizens that the tax distribution of the new system by income level is similar to the present one. The overriding concern is that we need more capital and then we need to make sure it is effectively invested in Iowa to build our jobs base and economic future of our communities.

Therefore, we must provide incentives for all citizens, regardless of income, to save and invest in this state's future. We need a tax policy that creates opportunities which make economic sense for all Iowans and outsiders to invest here in Iowa. In the new global economy, the good jobs, income and employment of the future will go where the investment goes.

6. Build on Strengths and Industries of the Future.

Agriculture is one of Iowa's major assets. We have some of the most productive land in the world. Agriculture will be here regardless of how much economic diversification we have. Rural policy research shows that rural areas have simply not done a very good job of attracting agricultural value-added plants into rural communities. Therefore, part of our investment resources must be devoted to adding value to Iowa's crops, livestock and rural communities. By developing new uses, new products and new markets, we can add value at home in Iowa's economy.

In addition to agriculture, Iowa must devote resources to diversifying its economic base. A balanced plan requires that some of both be done at the same time. A balanced plan requires that both urban and rural communities and their interests be given an opportunity to participate in Iowa's economic development efforts.

Iowa has had a statewide strategic plan since 1986, which attempts to target high-paying jobs and industries of the future. The Des Moines Chamber's recent Project 21 echoes Iowa's strategic plan and other efforts of the 1980s. Project 21 targets insurance, credit cards and data processing, biological production, value-added food production, food processing machinery manufacturing, and agribusiness product research.

While the thrust of these plans may be in an appropriate direction and some positive developments can be attributed to these efforts, the efforts have appeared to many as top down strategic planning processes. As a result, Iowans raise several questions. For example, do the outcomes reflect views of local participants from across the state or the project sponsors? If citizens want to create a level playing field for all communities and industries, is a statewide strategic plan that favors certain industries and communities over others needed? Do strategic plans become vehicles for passing favors to selected industry special interests? What happens to industry opportunities and community interests not in the strategic plan? Is there validity to reported relationships between economic development incentives and political contributions?

Such perceptions can cloud the usefulness of strategic plans and raise questions about whether we have gone too far down the road toward centralized planning by political and corporate elites. Perhaps Iowa citizens and community leaders would prefer improving the broad policy environment for Iowa's economy. A decentralized approach would focus more resources on local community and private sector development efforts that fit each of Iowa's diverse communities.

My view is that assisting public and private sector leaders in Iowa communities is the key to economic development. Each community effort contributes to Iowa's economic growth total. If local private and public sector leaders are unable to deliver, Iowa's economic growth does not happen.

Yes, worker retraining programs can help our state's businesses and workers adapt and move from mature industries to the value-added and target industries of the future. Iowa's universities and community colleges can play important roles in reaching these goals. But, the benefits must be distributed widely and not concentrated in one or two regions of the state. If the citizens on Main Street in Harlan or Maquoketa don't see the benefits from our collective research and economic development programs, they won't be interested in sending tax dollars to Des Moines to fund strategic plans.

7. Create a Level Playing Field for All.

The status quo approach in Iowa's economic development appears to be out-of-state business recruiting junkets, magazine promotions, and forgivable loans to companies that promise jobs. How many business leaders come to Iowa because they trust what our politicians told them at a reception? It takes more than promotion and marketing efforts to achieve maximum economic growth. Facts and a real growth environment must back up the marketing promotions to sustain success.

Have our leaders laid too many of our collective economic development eggs into quick-fix solutions like race tracks and riverboats? Risky decisions like fiber optics have been rushed at a time when we cannot afford mistakes. In each case, a few political leaders got together and rammed it through the political process without broad support of the people. While credit should be given for attempting to stimulate development, change also involves higher risks that can spell disaster.

Although the numbers vary from year to year, recent studies show 80 percent of new jobs being created by small businesses and most of these new jobs are created by expansion of existing community businesses. Is Iowa placing too much emphasis on recruiting out-of-state businesses? These numbers suggest that instead of central planning approaches to economic development, perhaps 80 percent of our resources ought to be targeted to supporting local community and business leaders in developing new markets and expanding home-grown and existing businesses.

On the other hand, state and local government units may have given too much away in some cases without adequate citizen input or input from other units of local government. It is true that state and local economic development tools have been successful in bringing development and jobs to many communities. However in the worst cases, an outside firm takes the tax breaks, brings in outside low-wage labor to fill the jobs, demands more local social services, increases property taxes for everyone else and then leaves town. Local existing businesses, city and county government, schools and taxpayers can all be impacted. If tax breaks are used in prospecting for outside firms, broad citizen input on the limits is needed before the prospecting begins.

In 1993, Iowa's leadership proposed two additional measures that go a step farther down the road of targeted preferential tax treatment: a property tax exemption on machinery and equipment purchased and an agricultural enterprise zone proposal. To receive the property tax exemption, a local city council or county board of supervisors would have to hold a public hearing and pass an ordinance. In the latter case, a petition with 50 signatures would be required to set up an agricultural enterprise zone and the qualifying livestock structures must increase the value of the property by more than 10 percent.

Over time, these approaches may create a "mine field" for economic development instead of a "level playing field." Both examples represent preferential tax treatment and departures from the principle of uniform and equal property taxation. The jobs tend to move toward counties with the deepest pockets. Counties deciding to keep more uniform and equal taxes are penalized.

These tax breaks often provide a competitive advantage to larger outside firms while penalizing existing taxpayers and smaller firms that have already made such investments. It is one thing for larger firms to proclaim greater economies of size based on efficiency. However, if we provide preferential tax treatment based on size or ability to threaten loss of jobs, we are favoring larger firms over small businesses, even though the smaller firms collectively account for most of the new jobs.

As a result, preferential subsidy proposals are divisive between outside businesses and existing businesses, between large businesses and small businesses, and businesses with ability to threaten jobs and those with long-term community loyalty. Wide-spread existence of such subsidies actually encourages firms to become more mobile and transient. Communities wishing to retain firms may have to contribute similar subsidies in order to prevent existing firms from moving out in the future. Preferential tax subsidies penalize firms who maintain long-term relationships with their home communities unless the same breaks are received.

Finally, when state and local politicians are required to approve every major local expansion effort, we create a bureaucratic system which slows the normal economic development process down. We also create a system that can be used unfairly to assure political patronage in future elections. "You approve my tax break and I'll contribute part of it to your next campaign." We create an environment where ethics issues are likely to arise on a regular basis.

Is there a way around these problems? Yes, there is. Why not consider a broader-based investment credit for all property taxpayers similar to those proposed for income taxes. Such a policy would be open to all local property taxpayers. Each could individually decide whether to save or invest in qualified enterprises. This contrasts to the other approaches which politicize the process and give preferential treatment in allocating local property tax breaks for economic development.

Another proposal that was initiated during the 1993 Legislative Session would provide state income tax free status for municipal bonds like the federal government does. We are in a period of historically low interest rates. Therefore, it may make economic sense for communities to think long-term and invest in rebuilding infrastructure. Iowa is one of a handful of states that does not provide tax free status for its own local municipal bonds. So, the proposal can be justified from that perspective. However, the proposal also provides preferential treatment for citizens who invest in the public sector over the private sector.

Instead of win-lose proposals that favor tax breaks for an elite group of interests or target capital to public sector projects only, we should develop win-win proposals that create incentives for all citizens—rich or poor, new or existing, insiders or outsiders, public or private—to save and invest in rebuilding Iowa's jobs base and economic future. That's a level playing field.

8. Negotiate Subsidy Limits For Attracting Business.

Major corporations, large and small, have spent a decade in mergers and consolidations buying out competition with junk bonds and providing golden parachutes to buy-off corporate executives. They have saddled consolidated businesses with mountains of debt and interest payments. The competitive positions of each state and the U.S. in international markets would have been far better off if the investments in mergers and consolidations had been spent on developing new products, new markets, new businesses, and expansion of existing firms.

Many of these same firms are now holding competing states and communities hostage to see who comes up with the biggest sweetheart deals before deciding new plant locations. As a result, the media would have us believe that perks, politics, and predatory business subsidies have become the main criteria for plant location instead of access to resources, cost of labor, productivity, access to markets, and comparative advantage.

During the recent bidding war for 1,000 to 1,200 Lennox jobs in Marshalltown, a new height in proposed corporate incentives was reached. Many Iowa communities end up paying about $8,000 to $10,000 per job to attract a new industry. After all was said and done, $18.5 million in direct incentives were provided by city, county, state, and private sector interests to keep Lennox. This amount represents about $16,000 per job.

The average pay will be about $9.00 per hour for an average annual salary of $18,500 before benefits. In addition, the community will benefit from added valuation and added spending in the community compared to the possibility of jobs lost, declining valuation, and reduced spending had Lennox moved. And since most of the incentives were loans, they will likely be repaid.

However, the direct incentives to Lennox are not what concern many Iowans. It is the other indirect incentives that were proposed by Iowa's political leadership. They promised a $25 million four-lane highway, offered passage of a workplace drug testing proposal favored by corporate CEOs, and passage of a $69 million machinery and equipment property tax credit proposal.

Iowa's political leaders publicly suggested these proposals were required to retain Lennox. Lennox officials denied that any of these three proposals were deal-breakers. However, the point is that Iowa's leadership created a precedent for any corporate CEO who controls a few hundred jobs to hold the location of the jobs hostage until special interest legislation clears the legislature. Such special interest pressure only encourages other CEOs to seek sweeter deals when raiding the public treasury in the future.

In many respects this issue is similar to the fundamental issues involved in the international arena among nations with debate over the General Agreement on Tariffs and Trade (GATT). In the absence of a general agreement, the marginal investment, plants, jobs, and trade go to the highest bidder with the deepest pockets and the biggest subsidies. These subsidies amount to a direct transfer from taxpayers, communities, and states to large multi-state and multi-national corporations. Enough is enough!

If each state spends most of its economic development resources on attracting businesses from other states, we collectively end up with less resources spent on developing new products, developing new markets, developing new firms, and expanding existing businesses in the U.S. as a whole. As a result, the United States becomes less competitive against international competition. Our world economic leadership erodes.

It's like the game of musical chairs. We spend all of our resources stealing each other's chairs instead of building more chairs. Pretty soon all of our chairs are gone. Iowa does not have the deepest pockets among the 50 states.

We cannot afford to get into a massive bidding war against other states for businesses that are holding the location of new plants hostage.

Instead of accelerating the interstate business subsidy wars as Iowa's leadership has done, Iowa should take the lead in negotiating interstate compacts to eliminate the predatory business subsidies and to define a set of rules for growing more businesses and strengthening our collective competitiveness. If we do this, the U.S. and each of the 50 states will be stronger in the international marketplace in the longer run.

Caution is needed however. Decelerating the interstate subsidy wars may require Iowa to match or increase subsidies of other states in the short run. This may seem contradictory, but it is not. It is similar to the U.S. strategy of increasing export subsidies in the short run to pressure the Europeans at the GATT negotiating table. If we unilaterally disarm our subsidies, we harm our own economy and other states benefit. Therefore, we must be prepared to continue and possibly increase our subsidies until a multi-state agreement is finalized.

9. Avoid False Solutions: Taxpayer's Rights Amendment.

Proponents of the Taxpayer's Rights Amendment have pushed the measure for years claiming Constitutional limits on government spending fosters fiscal responsibility, efficiency, and economic growth in Iowa. However, a recent study by three education groups provided evidence that if the version of the Taxpayer's Rights Amendment proposed in the 1993 General Assembly was actually passed, the impacts would likely be opposite of the promises.

The Taxpayer's Rights Amendment would place limits on revenue growth for all state and local units of government beyond those that already exist. The formula would peg each taxing unit to a base year of revenue. Future revenue growth would be limited by the base year average revenue per person times local population growth and inflation. For school districts, student enrollment is used as the population indicator.

What are the economic impacts? The key finding from the preliminary study is that nearly two-thirds of the statewide impacts are in Iowa's ten largest and fastest growing counties. As a result, economic growth may in fact be slowed down by the proposed amendment. This occurs because the cost of adding additional services and capacity in growing communities is almost always greater than the pre-existing average cost per person times added population and inflation. Impacts would be even greater during rapid economic expansion and low inflation.

Iowa's ten largest counties account for 45 percent of the state's population. To maintain Iowa's present slow growth economy, we collectively depend on rapid growth in the fastest growing counties to offset declines in other areas of the state. Therefore the amendment would likely slow Iowa's economic growth.

The national indicators used in the formula can change rapidly from year to year. They are often more reflective of events on the east and west coasts. Ten to 25 percent of the time, Iowa's economy is heating up or cooling off when the national economy is doing the opposite. If we base next year's state and local government revenue limits on last year's national indicators, we may constrain local economic growth precisely during times when it needs to be stimulated, and we may stimulate local growth at other times when it is not needed.

Also, communities with similar economic growth rates would not necessarily be affected the same by the formula. Industrial expansion drives the need for government service expansion in some communities. But nearby, we often see a growing bedroom community that counts all of the population boom. The amendment would penalize the community with industrial expansion but reward the bedroom community whose residents fill the jobs.

The amendment requires an accurate population count for each taxing unit. While annual population surveys are conducted by the Census Bureau, we really only get an accurate population count every decade. The Census Bureau may not provide annual projections for cities under 2,500. Iowans for Tax Relief, the sponsor of the amendment, suggested using the population growth rate from the previous decade. This would adversely limit small communities that were sleepy a decade ago, but are now rapidly growing. In the final analysis, more staff would be required if we are to calculate population growth and limits accurately for each of the 1,500 cities, counties, and local districts each year.

The proposed amendment would duplicate and sometimes contradict the existing spending controls in place on local government. Taxes for Iowa's local government units have only increased 47 percent between 1982 and 1990, compared to 66 percent for state government. When present tax rate limits are reached, it takes a vote of the people to raise more revenue. It appears that existing local limits have worked fairly well. At the state level, only time will tell whether the new state budget processes and renewed pledges of fiscal responsibility by Iowa's political leaders are successful. If they do their job, adding another formula adds more government bureaucracy.

Would it control government spending? A study by the National Conference of State Legislatures evaluated the effectiveness of the tax and expenditure limits that presently exist in 19 states. They concluded such limits have been generally ineffective in controlling the growth of state government in comparison to other states. While such limits have been somewhat effective in controlling local government growth, Iowa already has implemented local revenue limits. Therefore, we might expect less effective impacts in Iowa. Local government is not where the deficits have occurred in Iowa.

Because the Constitution is difficult to change, it is our responsibility as citizens to evaluate closely Constitutional Amendments which can have unintended impacts 25, 50 and 100 years down the road. Future circumstances may turn out differently from those expected. Anecdotal reports of local service dislocations and economic growth constraints in some California communities after Proposition 13 provides justification for thorough study and full debate before similar limits are passed in Iowa. Perhaps the amendment ought to be voluntarily tested in a few counties before it is applied to the rest of the state.

Finally if the amendment was passed, it would not become effective until after the next election. Simply put, it is a convenient political maneuver that allows status quo politicians to be perceived as being fiscally responsible without making hard decisions in resolving the budget issues at hand. In reality it shifts the public focus off of the real causes and solutions to the current Iowa budget crisis and debate.

Iowa citizens should focus attention on electing fiscally responsible leaders, solving the current budget crisis, improving our bond ratings, and restoring the current Constitutional sections on balancing the budget that have been ignored for a decade. These actions would improve Iowa's economic development environment and do not carry the risks of eroding Iowa's future economic growth like passing the 1993 Taxpayer's Rights Amendment.

If Iowans cannot enforce the balanced budget provisions already in Iowa's Constitution, we have little justification for adding new and more complex amendments for which the impacts are less clear and potentially harmful to economic growth. Why penalize or constrain future generations of Iowans for mistakes and fiscal irresponsibility of the present generation of leaders?

10. People with Courage to Take Responsibility.

In the final analysis, status quo leaders don't want to talk about the erosion of Iowa's economic position or major reforms. It would mean they have failed in their responsibility. It upsets the cozy relationships that have developed with elite special interests. It reduces the chances for re-election.

In recent years our state's vitality and pride have been tarnished. Somehow, we have gotten off track. The question is, will we continue the erosion with status quo economic policy or will we have the courage to change? Will we accept leaving this state in worse condition for the next generation?

Iowa can be a great state again. We can restore our pride. Citizens can increase our stake in Iowa's future. It won't be easy. But we are people who work hard and smart. We can do almost anything we pledge our talents, time, and resources to. We don't want to leave Iowa in a mess for the next generation.

But to accomplish success in rebuilding our jobs base, Iowans must be bold. We must change our course. We must prudently manage our resources and we must start investing in our future like we have never invested before.

That's it. There's no secret to Japanese or German successes. They simply invested at a rate two to three times greater than the U.S. for the past three decades and their governments worked more closely with the private sectors to nurture, develop, and acquire strategic industries.

We can do the same thing. We can make ourselves more attractive by reforming our economic policy. If we do, we will demonstrate to the nation how it can be done. In the process, we will restore our pride. We will rebuild our jobs base. We will create economic opportunity for the next generation.

Chapter 2. Restoring Fiscal Responsibility.

1. Iowa's Constitution: Ignored for a Decade.

The Constitution should be the most respected document in a democracy because it defines our most basic democratic principles and institutions of government. The Constitution defines the political powers and responsibilities retained by the citizenry and those transferred to elected officials, and government institutions. In a democracy, the most fundamental principle is that the people retain supreme political power.

Thomas Jefferson and other founders felt the Constitution, in particular, should be written in language that common citizens could understand. If the Constitution is widely read, understood, and supported by the people, then the people can defend it against abuses of power. Therefore, the people not only retain supreme political power in a democracy, they are also ultimately responsible for defending the principles outlined in the Constitution from potential abuses of power when they occur.

So, when we start to analyze what went wrong in the creation of Iowa's budget deficit, we must start with a better understanding of Iowa's Constitution. What does Iowa's Constitution say about fiscal responsibility and budget deficits? It states the following principle:

> "Article VII. State Debts: Section 2. Limitation: The State may contract debts to supply casual deficits or failures in revenues, or to meet expenses not otherwise provided for; but the aggregate amount of such debts, direct and contingent, whether contracted by virtue of one or more acts of the General Assembly, or at different periods of time, shall never exceed the sum of two hundred and fifty thousand dollars and the money arising from the creation of such debts, shall be applied to the purpose for which it was obtained, or to repay the debts so contracted, and to no other purposes whatever."

I have asked Iowa leaders and citizens across the state to read this section of the Iowa Constitution and tell me what it means. They say it means that our state has a balanced budget amendment already in the Constitution. It says we should not borrow more than $250,000 for deficits, so we shouldn't have a budget deficit greater than $250,000 either.

Then I ask if this is something they agree with? In almost every case, they say yes, we should have a balanced budget and it is a good idea to have it written in the Constitution. Usually without prompting, they add that if the Constitution says this, how did we end up with a $409 million dollar deficit?

In a nutshell, political leadership in both parties has simply ignored the Constitution and views of Iowa citizens regarding Constitutional intent. Legalese and rhetoric have been used to turn what would otherwise be a black and white issue into something that is gray.

2. How Did the Deficit Develop? Who is Responsible?

Does anyone think Iowa's budget deficit magically occurred over night? Some experts point to 1989 as the start of our current deficit problems. A few experts go back as far as 1978. That was the year Iowa began to accelerate collections of Iowa business taxes to improve its cash flow. Most experts, including the State Auditor and State Treasurer, trace the root of Iowa's budget problems to the practice of accruing next year's tax revenues to balance this year's budget. This practice began in 1983, when $112.7 million was accrued from 1984 revenue collections to balance the 1983 budget. The amount of annually accrued revenues has grown every year since 1983 to 1993.

Who was in charge? The practice of accruing revenues to balance the budget was invented during the first year of the Branstad Administration and the Branstad Administration has presided over the budget every year since revenues were first accrued in 1983.

An anecdote from *United We Stand* sums up the relationship between our political leaders and budget deficits. "Its like the family with a crazy aunt who lives down stairs. Everybody knows she is there. But nobody wants to admit they are responsible." Or if they do, they quickly change the subject and hope that we forget about their responsibility as soon as possible. But the fact is, it happened on their watch. Yes, Iowa was under financial pressure at the time due to the farm crisis and new federalism. Yes, accruing revenues started out small. Yes, like a glass of whiskey to an alcoholic, it got harder to refuse the next drink. The practice compounded itself. We used next year's revenue to balance this year's budget, so it became harder to balance next year's budget. Bankers and farmers who went through the farm debt crisis carrying one year's operating loans over to the next year for several years in a row are very familiar with the consequences of compounding operating debts over many years.

At the end of the 1980s, Iowa's legislative leadership acted in a manner which seemed to presume our economy had bounced back stronger than before the farm crisis and recession. While Iowa's economy and state revenues bounced back some in 1989 and 1990, Iowa never fully recovered from the farm crisis. However, the Legislature with the Governor's approval rapidly increased state spending at a rate more than double the revenue growth.

In 1989 and 1990, the Legislature and Governor initiated several new multi-year spending programs, including fiber optics, optional medicaid, environmental programs, and prison expansions. The programs were passed before it was clear that revenue expectations would not be reached. By 1992, the State Auditor announced that his list of new programs passed since 1987 was "41 pages long!"

In 1990 and 1991, the Legislature and Governor also set up lease-purchase agreements under the Department of Corrections to finance two prison expansions and under the General Services Department to build the fiber optics network. What is different about these actions? In each case, securities called certificates of participation were sold to raise funds for the construction projects. And in each case, state general funds were pledged to pay off part of the certificates.

It sounds a lot like borrowing and using general funds to pay the interest and principal on the debt—only it isn't called debt. Instead, it is called a lease payment. Experts suggest the whole process was invented to circumvent deficit and debt restrictions in Iowa's Constitution. Whether such certificates constitute debt and whether they are constitutional has never been tested before Iowa's Supreme Court.

State government may not be the only ones using the creative debt instruments to bypass legal debt limits. Similar lease-purchase agreements are apparently sometimes used by local governments to get around local debt limits and bond issues requiring a public vote. Iowa has one of the lowest levels of bonded debt of any state. Many interests make a case that it is appropriate to create public debt to finance long-term capital projects that increase productivity over several decades.

However, no wonder Iowans are frustrated with government. So many state and local officials appear willing to skirt the limits with creative debt instruments instead of going through the democratic process of raising the limits or formally changing the rules of the game.

How many families and businesses stay out of financial trouble if they go on a spending spree with their credit cards before they know what their annual income is going to be? Poor financial management led to a need for the continued use of creative accounting practices and creative debt instruments. Creative accounting and creative debt were necessary for the Governor and Legislative leaders to fund programs on their respective agendas without obviously violating the Constitution.

In recent months it has been suggested that Iowa is on track toward having the best managed state budget in the nation. This conclusion was based on the idea that Iowa has taken most of the annual spending off automatic pilot; we have limited spending to 99 percent of revenue projections; and we have set up a "rainy day fund." Maybe a decade from now it will be true.

However, this pronouncement overlooks the assertion that Iowa could have said the same thing a decade ago. In contrast to our federal government, Iowa already had a balanced budget amendment in our Constitution. Unlike the President of the United States, Iowa's Governor already had a line item veto. As a result, every dollar that Iowa has spent for the past decade in creating our state budget crisis can be equally attributed to the Governor and the Legislature.

3. Creative Accounting Becomes Conflict of Interest.

The Administration has reported an end-of-year "legal balance" surplus of $0 to $96 million for each year since 1983. If the accrued revenues are subtracted, the general fund balance would have shown deficits ranging from $86 to $264 million at the end of each year since 1983 (See Charts).

Interpretation of state law suggests that any general fund legal balance deficit requires a statewide property tax levy to cover the shortfall. Political leaders claim the political problems caused by collecting a statewide property tax almost assures us that it will never be tried. So, a strong incentive exists for ending the year with a positive "legal balance."

Standards for state "legal balances" are passed by the Iowa Legislature and interpreted by the Governor while Generally Accepted Accounting Principles (GAAP) are set by a national board of professional accountants. Historically, it has not been uncommon for states to adopt their own "legal balance" system for accounting. However as more states began to borrow in national credit markets, the financial industry developed GAAP standards so the financial status of all states could be uniformly evaluated for credit worthiness. As a result, many states have begun to keep two sets of books.

In the mid-1980s, Iowa policymakers adopted a phase-in plan to replace the present "legal balances" accounting system with GAAP standards. In 1987, Iowa had an estimated GAAP deficit of $195 million. Iowa adopted targets for reducing the 1987 GAAP deficit by 10 to 20 percent per year over six years. It was to be eliminated by 1993. Well, it didn't happen. We began to miss the targets by the end of the 1990 fiscal year.

By July 1992, GAAP accounting showed a deficit of $409 million, but the Administration reported a "legal balance" of $2 million for the same year. The GAAP deficit was estimated to come down to $337 million by July 1993. However, without figuring sales tax increases imposed in July 1992, Iowa's 1993 GAAP deficit would have been $600 million.

Using Iowa's accounting standards for "legal balances" normally does not present a problem as long as the same

Figure 1.

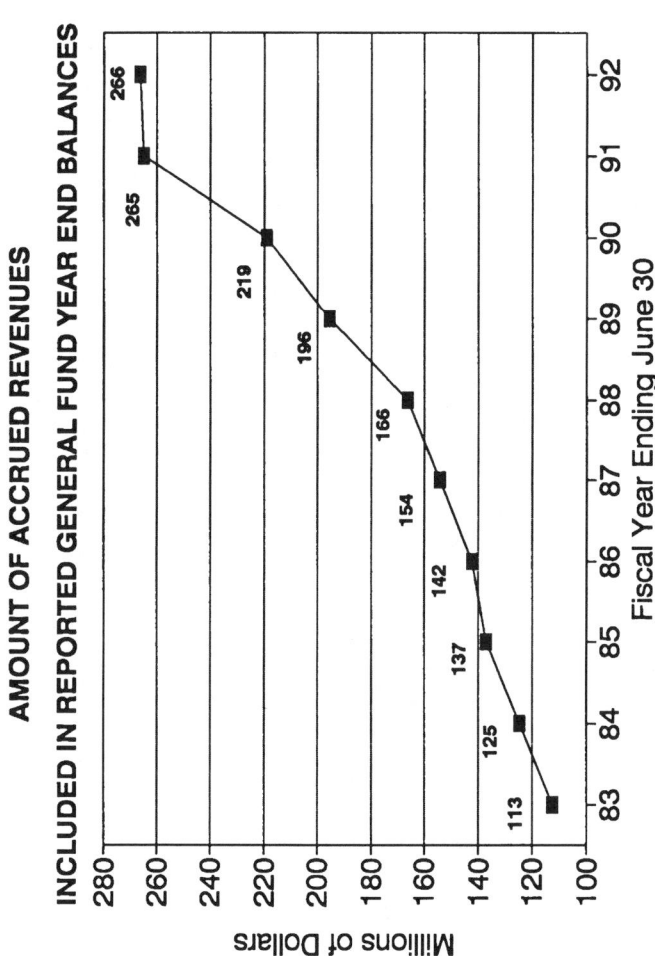

Figure 2.

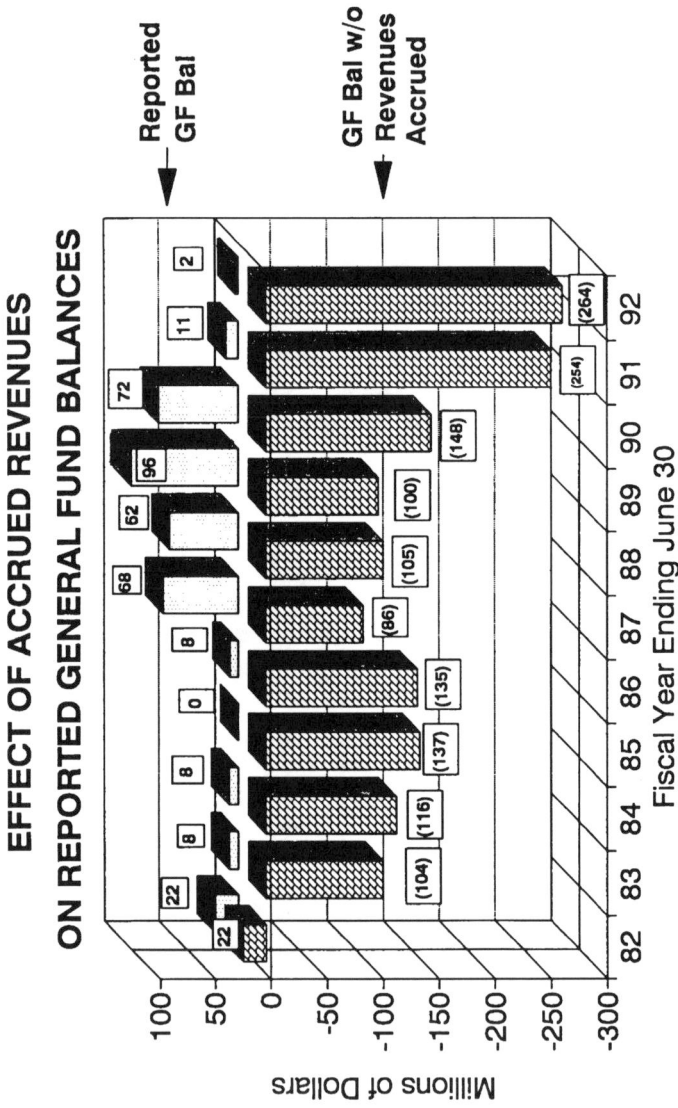

Figure 3.

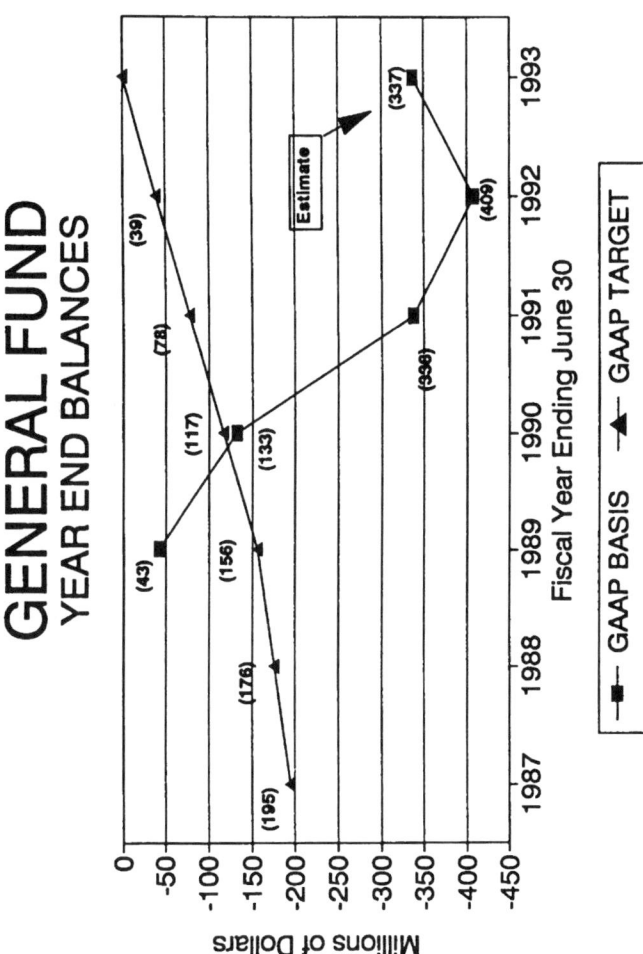

accounting rules and practices are followed each year. However, serious questions have been periodically raised because the practices have been changed year to year. In 1991, the Republican State Auditor and Democrat State Treasurer publicly charged that the accounting practices used to calculate the "legal balances" were being altered from year to year by the Administration in response to Iowa's cash flow problems. And, the legislative leadership appeared to have gone along with the creative accounting in its budgeting process.

As a result, most financial and budget experts have come to regard Iowa's legal balance as "smoke and mirrors." Because questions have arisen regarding the accounting practices, GAAP standards are now perceived by many Iowans as the ethical way for Iowa to keep its books in the future.

Since many of the problems that contributed to Iowa's budget crisis can be traced to spending decisions made in 1989 and 1990, the possibility is raised that the Governor and his opponent, the former Speaker of the House, gained politically in the 1990 election campaign due to less than full public disclosure of Iowa's budget crisis. Both candidates played leadership roles in passing state spending increases and new programs signed into law during the 1989 and 1990 General Assembly. In turn, these spending increases created the GAAP deficits in 1990 and 1991.

Neither candidate had an incentive to raise the budget issue during the 1990 gubernatorial campaign. Both had opportunity to include special favors for target voting groups in the 1990 legislative session, knowing the results would not show up until after the election in the budget for 1990-91 fiscal year.

Citizens can raise serious questions about the public's right to know if partisan politics were given higher priority than accuracy in public information during the developing budget crisis. During the recent campaigns, the media reported gag orders on state government employees regarding the release of information that might have negative campaign consequences. A month after the campaign was over, the media reported that a large increase in the deficit would appear by June 31, 1991. That year, Iowa's GAAP deficit grew by $205 million over the previous year.

It was also during the Fall of 1990 that the state union contract negotiations began, which concluded with an independent arbitrator siding with the state union on a 9 percent salary increase over two years. The salary decision is not surprising in retrospect. The information available on the condition of the state budget led most citizens to believe we were in good shape. Large spending increases had been passed by the two previous General Assemblies and signed by the Governor.

The point is that responsibility for the $409 million GAAP deficit does not totally rest on Democrats who controlled the Legislature for the past 10 years or the Republican Governor who chose not to use the line item veto. Both were party to the management style that created the deficit crisis. Thus, both are responsible for the largest tax increase in Iowa's history.

A couple of years of fiscal responsibility may or may not make up for a decade of skirting the Constitution and presiding over the creation of the largest budget crisis in state history. Evidence suggests accounting practices were still being changed at the end of fiscal year 1992. State Auditor reports show that trust funds supposedly separate from the General Fund were "cleaned out" to help balance the budget on June 30, 1992.

4. The Would-Be Defenders of Iowa's Constitution.

Is the present accounting system used to calculate Iowa's "legal balances" constitutional? During the Fall of 1991, the State Auditor asked for an Attorney General's opinion regarding several Administration accounting practices. The opinions handed down stated that changing the accounting practices from year to year was questionable. However, in spite of the questionable accounting practice changes, the present system was presumed to be "legal" for accounting purposes. Thus the Attorney General, who also has expressed gubernatorial aspirations, effectively stopped what could have been a legitimate constitutional challenge of Iowa's accounting practices.

Perhaps it might help to reread the Constitution and redraw your own conclusions about the intent of the drafters. It appears to be written as tightly as citizens could write concerning a fundamental accounting principle. Interpreting Iowa's Constitution involves more than an interpretation of the statutes. It involves interpretation of intent of the fundamental economic and accounting principles in the Constitution and judgment regarding their implementation.

The Iowa Supreme Court is the final judge of constitutional intent. Since the Supreme Court Justices have been appointed by Governors with party affiliations different from the Attorney General, some citizens might conclude the Supreme Court's view of Iowa's Constitution might be different from the Attorney General's opinion. However to date, Iowa's creative accounting and debt practices have not been tested in Iowa's Supreme Court.

The Attorney General could have taken charge in a campaign to protect Iowa citizens and the Constitution from a potential abuse of power. She did not. The Attorney General had an opportunity to demonstrate stronger fiscal leadership than either the Governor or her own party's Legislative leadership by restoring fiscal responsibility in the middle of Iowa's worst budget crisis in history, but she did not.

Additional opportunities to restore fiscal responsibility developed when Iowans for Tax Relief filed suits to test the constitutionality of Iowa's budget deficits in 1991 and 1992. However, neither case was ever tested on its merits. Both suits were thrown out on procedural grounds. Essentially, the judges decided the suits were brought against the wrong state officials.

In the first case, the judge dismissed the suit because it was brought against the Executive Council. The second suit was dismissed because it named the State Treasurer. The state contends that the Department of Management and Department of Revenue are the appropriate agencies which should have been named. The judge sided with the State and decided the Treasurer's official responsibilities were not germane to the issues and charges raised in the suit. In fact, he and the State Auditor were the two state officials who raised concerns about Iowa's questionable accounting practices a year earlier.

Therefore, the evidence suggests either Iowans for Tax Relief should consider naming the appropriate parties in future suits or perhaps Iowans for Tax Relief have other lobbying strategies and priorities in mind.

What might the other strategies be? Iowans for Tax Relief was the largest contributor to 1992 legislative campaigns and sponsor of the Taxpayer's Rights Amendment outlined in the previous chapter. These facts create an opportunity for developing a classic political straddle strategy.

How does a straddle work? In a commodities or stock market straddle, the investor identifies two similar contracts or stocks. The investor will go long on one and short on the other when they have reason to believe that the trends between the two investments will widen or narrow. If the investor can influence the profitability of one of the firms, they have even greater potential opportunity to profit from the straddle.

Similarly, Iowans opposed to creative accounting and creative debt practices, want fiscal responsibility restored. Testing the present Constitution and proposing a new more limiting constitutional amendment are two strategies that are similarly perceived to restore fiscal responsibility. The most straight forward approach is to test the current provisions in Iowa's Constitution. However, by pushing procedurally flawed Supreme Court challenges, other groups are less inclined to file their suits and the normal citizen remedy for restoring fiscal responsibility is derailed. As citizen frustration increases, public support shifts toward the similar but more radical approach to limit government and restore fiscal responsibility.

When the most recent suit was dismissed in early 1992, Iowans for Tax Relief threatened but did not immediately refile their suit against the officials with responsibility for the practices covered by the suit. However, the Governor added the Taxpayer's Rights Amendment, also sponsored by Iowans for Tax Relief, to his legislative agenda for solving the budget crisis at the end of the 1992 General Assembly and first Special Session of 1992.

The Governor then dropped the Taxpayer's Rights Amendment from his budget crisis agenda before the end of the second Special Session. However instead of resubmitting a suit naming the appropriate Administration officials who were responsible for the creative accounting, Iowans for Tax Relief appealed the previously dismissed suit which still named the State Treasurer at fault. Therefore, the Supreme Court will rule during the Fall of

1993 on whether the suit was brought against the appropriate state officials. They may not rule on whether Iowa's creative accounting was constitutional. If not, three years will have been lost without testing the merits of the case and citizens still won't know what Iowa's Constitution means.

A Supreme Court challenge on the constitutionality of creative accounting and creative debt still has merit. Citizens should encourage Iowans for Tax Relief or other "good" government groups to push a legitimate suit. Iowa's existing constitutional remedies for fiscal irresponsibility should not be held hostage in seeking passage of more radical measures. A successful Supreme Court test of Iowa's Constitution would help end speculation that Iowans for Tax Relief is using the political straddle strategy to generate support for its Taxpayer's Rights Amendment. While the two failed suits are not proof of a straddle, a third failed appeal would represent a pattern.

Iowa citizens need to know once and for all how Iowa's Supreme Court interprets the existing Constitution. If the Court decides creative accounting and creative debt practices are not legal, then state officials would have to immediately balance the budget. If the Court decides the practices are legal, citizens then could begin working on a constitutional amendment that would put stronger and clearer balanced budget language into Iowa's Constitution. Iowa's political leadership could not ignore the Constitution as they have the past decade.

If a legitimate Supreme Court challenge doesn't develop, the last resort in protecting Iowa's Constitution is the court of public opinion by citizens in future elections. For the common person who reads Iowa's Constitution and takes his or her responsibility for protecting it seriously, confidence and credibility of state government will not likely be restored until the GAAP deficit is eliminated by responsible politicians who follow the rules.

5. Priority One: Balance the Budget.

Iowa's first priority must be to balance the budget and eliminate the GAAP deficit. We cannot reposition and rebuild our jobs base for the future until we have the present budget crisis behind us. The GAAP deficit must be eliminated. Status quo politicians tried to eliminate it once before in the 1980s and failed. In 1992, we passed another plan to eliminate the GAAP deficit over three years by 1995. Already, there has been discussion about circumstances for postponing the present plan.

A recent court decision may cost Iowa an estimated $42 to $70 million to settle claims with federal retirees and corporate tax withholding because Iowa illegally taxed federal retirees, but not state retirees. In addition, Iowa was declared a statewide disaster area due to the record floods of 1993.

The state must shoulder it's responsibility and pay it's share of the bill for collective damage prevention, assuring public safety, repairing infrastructure, and clean up. The flood may impose a loss in revenue and significant expenditure on the state budget. Because of this emergency, some will say, "Let's postpone eliminating Iowa's GAAP deficit." If we do, the total cost of the emergency should be laid on top of the table for all citizens to see. Unlike last time, the deficit elimination plan must not be extended for three years if the total cost of the emergency only requires one. If Iowa fails to make progress in balancing the budget this time, our state is likely to lose the opportunity to restore confidence in government. And, our state's economic future is at stake.

6. Priority Two: No More Tax Increases.

Iowa's second priority should be to balance the budget without increasing the total collective tax effort of Iowans any further. In the short run, there are only two ways to eliminate the GAAP deficit: raise the growth in revenue or cut the growth in spending. In 1992, we imposed the largest tax increase in Iowa history. We cannot afford another tax increase next term.

In fact, a Public Policy Education Focus Group of leaders from diverse interests across Iowa concluded the sales tax hike passed in 1992 should only be imposed on a temporary basis for three years. Once the GAAP deficit has been paid off and Iowa's cash flow situation replenished, the Focus Group suggested that reducing the sales tax should be placed back on the table for debate with all the other proposals for increasing government spending.

Why should Iowa automatically spend funds originally pledged to deficit reduction after the deficit is paid off?

Clearly the emphasis must be placed on reducing the rate of increase in spending growth and shifting the tax mix in ways that encourage all Iowans to participate in rebuilding Iowa's jobs base. As a state, we must continue to make hard choices that involve setting our priorities and slowing spending growth to match revenue growth. Status quo politicians usually back away from the hard choices unless they are forced into it.

Yet, most individuals face these hard choices every day. Can I afford a new car? Do the kids really need those new clothes? What should we pay the babysitter? Should I pay down my Master Charge card? What are we going to do about those bank overdrafts? These are everyday decisions that don't involve philosophy or ideology, but they do require prudent management.

Citizens make these decisions every day. We should expect no less from political leaders. Ask the status quo politician if he or she wants more money for education or health care. They quickly calculate who gives them what and how it will look to constituents. They answer we want both, and then they blame the tax increases on the other party. This is an answer we can no longer afford.

We must recognize the budget will require tough decisions every year for the next several years. Most politicians thought they solved the budget problems with the two special sessions in 1992. And indeed, progress was made. The proportion of Iowa General Fund spending on automatic pilot went from 60 percent down to 12 percent. The legislature limited its expenditures to 99 percent of expected revenues. A rainy day fund was set up and property tax limits were placed on counties and cities. However, Iowa state government still increased spending by $260 million, which was more than double the expected normal growth in state revenues that would have occurred without the sales tax hike.

For fiscal 1993, only about $75 million of the $240 million sales tax hike was allocated to GAAP deficit reduction. The remaining $170 million in new sales tax revenues was added to the $90 million in normal revenue growth. In total, $260 million was allocated to increased state spending and ending balances.

According to the Department of Management, 39 percent of the new spending went to salary increases, 39 percent went to K-12 school aid, and 22 percent to Medicaid. All other state agencies and departments received no net increase in operating budgets. For some this meant no change for a second year in a row.

7. Prioritize Discretionary Spending.

We have turned our public sector managers into glorified bean counters. Currently, if they are given a choice, most public managers would give all employees the same raise and would reward all programs the same regardless of outcomes and performance. This allows managers to sit in a safe position and collect large salaries for pushing paper for higher-ups.

However just like the private sector, not all public employees generate the same results. Not all programs generate significant outcomes. Innovative programs are often canceled to protect status quo interests. In many respects, managers and employees down in the trenches are in the best position to identify unnecessary, inefficient, or outdated programs. They are also in the best position to identify new areas of need to be serviced if funds were reallocated. Their input on priorities not only deserves respect but should be required and made public along with their budget requests.

All managers of departments and agencies of Iowa's state and local government should periodically be required to identify the lowest priority programs in their agency equal to five percent of their budget requests. If they try to play games by identifying the priority programs with broad appeal, their superiors have grounds for finding new managers.

In addition, managers should be asked to submit innovative proposals that would improve productivity, efficiency, and serve new priority needs. In developing the agency priorities at the grassroots level, better management practices including principles of strategic planning, customer satisfaction, and employee satisfaction would be encouraged.

High performance institutions pay attention to managers and employees down in the trenches. In fact, many high performance institutions regard those in trenches as the most important employees in the system. They are the ones who serve the citizens.

In the absence of sound management and constituent information systems, policymakers have little information for judging public sector performance and priorities other than to respond to raw political pressure. This political pressure often comes from the special interest groups with the greatest organizational skills, deepest pockets, and strongest relationships with the legislative leadership.

Perhaps the best example of a discretionary program that could have been slowed down is the fiber optics network. Cost efficient technology should be adopted. However, a statewide fiber optics network is a huge undertaking of an untested concept for a state facing the worst financial crisis in its history.

In contrast, we didn't rush building the whole interstate highway system. We did it over a longer period of years. As we experimented with highways, we found out that we didn't need an interstate highway to every county seat. The long run benefits of fiber optics may yet develop and put Iowa at the cutting edge of communications technology. It may yet bring high-paying jobs to Iowa. To date, however, its superior usefulness has not been widely demonstrated. As a result, the demand for the system and its cost effectiveness remain in serious question. As one analyst put it, "...it appears that only a half a dozen people in the whole state really wanted the fiber optics system."

Regardless of the ultimate benefits of fiber optics to Iowa, the ends do not necessarily justify the means. Fiber optics provides a case example of ways in which status quo politicians misuse political power which in turn generate negative impacts on Iowa's budget. The Administration and Legislative leadership pushed the fiber optics proposal through during the last three days of the session when they knew policymakers would be very busy and when they also knew that procedural rules would allow passage without having a fiscal note on the total cost of the system for legislators to consider.

Then, the Administration rushed the construction and bidding process of the fiber optics contracts before the Governor's own Commission on Spending Reform could effectively review whether the project should have been postponed, slowed down, or terminated. In the final analysis, the only remedy for stopping such abuses of political power is to replace leadership that is prone toward such abuses with leadership that is not.

8. Smooth Out Erratic Salary Increases.

It used to be that many people were attracted to employment in the public sector out of a desire to serve the public. Public employees were held to a higher standard of conduct and ethics than their private sector counterparts. Public employees took pride in their work and satisfaction in accomplishing something good in service to society. This standard of professionalism has been eroded in Iowa by poor management and politicization of the public sector. We must restore pride for service to the public. We must lead public sector professionals by challenge and respect and not by mandate, belittlement, or ruling decree.

Freezing public employee salaries one year and then turning around to give large raises is a poor management strategy for generating a highly productive and high performance public sector. Outstanding employees are penalized during freezes. Large raises create opportunities for administrative abuse, distortions, and rewards beyond employee productivity. Employees conclude that raises are more a matter of politics instead of being related to their job performance.

The Administration cannot make threats to privatize state jobs or bring suit against public employees and claim to create a highly productive work environment at the same time. The Supreme Court agreed the Administration violated the intent of the collective bargaining law. While deficit reduction is an honorable goal, public employees were used as a scapegoat for the previous deficit decisions and fiscal problems of the Legislature and Administration.

As a general rule, public employee salaries should grow no more rapidly than the general growth in the economy and growth in state budget revenues. On the other hand, state employees should not be punished with zero salary increases as a result of policymaker overspending and fiscal mismanagement. Iowa needs a standardized process and a consistent policy that is fair to all concerned. The system should take into account a number of factors, including performance of the employee, customer satisfaction, job market conditions, and cost of living.

Unions grow primarily due to failures of management. When the management treats workers poorly, unions gain strength. We have seen state lawsuits against unions fail. We have seen weak efforts to privatize state entities that may not generate great savings when all is said and done. The media provides the perception that government is trampling over the little guys who aren't making much anyway. As a result, it would appear that Iowa is following the best strategy for growing bigger unions.

In other states, there is a philosophy that management should treat workers decently and fairly. If management does this, then workers will be less inclined to organize because the workers won't have any reason for doing so.

Finally, many of Iowa's public institutions have turned into top down organizations with a more politicized management style. There is a need for managers to be evaluated from the bottom up. Iowa should return to participatory management styles that systematically gather customer and employee input on performance. If we really want total quality management, managers must challenge, encourage, reward, and listen to employees.

9. Isolate and Examine Entitlement Costs.

The bi-partisan welfare reforms proposed during the 1993 General Assembly represent a step in the right direction toward providing aid to those who cannot provide for their own needs, controlling entitlement costs, and trying to move people into more productive lifestyles. If we have too many people riding in the boat but not rowing, we will only progress at a slow pace. Those who have criticized the program have not criticized its intent; they have criticized the lack of funding support and jobs commitment required for successful implementation. If we are going to reform the system, we better do it right.

In addition, we must continue to monitor Medicaid costs. Iowa Medicaid entitlements have been growing at 10 to 20 percent while Iowa's revenue growth is growing at 4 to 6 percent. According to the Department of

Management, if no changes are made, Medicaid is expected to take 65 percent of Iowa's annual growth in revenues by 1996. State government has been screwed down tightly for two years; it is not out of the woods yet.

Medicaid entitlements cannot be allowed to continue to erode the other important functions of government or erode Iowa's tax base and income generating capacity. Yet such choices are sometimes more complex than they seem. For every dollar spent on Medicaid, Iowa receives two additional federal dollars. This kind of return is higher than most private sector investments. As a result, Iowa cannot cut Medicaid programs without a negative impact on retaining dollars in Iowa's economy. We need to make sure that we are accomplishing what we intend.

The general functions of government and the competitiveness of the private sector must not be jeopardized by federal government incentives for expanding optional entitlements. Those who most directly benefit should pay part of the bill. For example, if we make eye glasses free under Medicaid, there should be a disincentive for breaking them every now and then just to get a more stylish pair. It is a basic economic principle that people will take more when they are spending other people's money. Therefore, all capable adults who receive benefits should provide a contribution or share some of the costs.

At the same time, we must remember that two-thirds of the people on welfare are children. We have many more single parent households today than three decades ago. There appears to be consensus that investment in parenting skills and early childhood education prevents higher cost problems down the road.

As a result, Iowa's reform efforts require a balancing act. Clearly, instead of programs with highly specified rules by higher levels of government, we need pilot programs designed to assist communities in solving problems faced by families and individuals who truly cannot provide for their own needs. By combining various state and federal aid funds under the control of local community boards, local leaders could solve community problems and provide accountability for individual and family contracts.

For example, unemployment, economic development, job training, child care, and welfare funds could be combined in a community-based program to match unemployed persons with certain skills and capital-poor start up firms. This would move people off welfare, provide training, and encourage economic development at the same time. Of course, there are several variations that could be tried. Rather than debating philosophical merits of the proposals and forcing the state to adopt one big plan to fit all communities, perhaps we should pilot test the ideas and let local communities find out what works under various conditions.

10. Reform and Reduce Property Taxes.

Iowa presently ranks in the top third among states in terms of property tax effort in relation to our tax burden. The tax model of the Iowa Legislative Fiscal Bureau indicates that Iowa's property tax is regressive. Almost all surveys of Iowa citizens in recent years have indicated they want property taxes lowered. It is time we listened to the people. We need to examine ways to make Iowa's property taxes less regressive. We need to lower the proportion of property taxes in Iowa's tax mix.

In recent years, Iowa has drifted away from the principle of uniform and equal taxation of property according to its highest and best legal use. Today, only a few people in the state appear to know that Iowa property taxes have become severely distorted by a hidden assessment rollback calculation. In 1992, all residential property in Iowa received a 27.4 percent assessment rollback. This arbitrarily shifts a quarter of the local residential property tax burden to commercial, industrial, and agricultural property. In other words, more than a quarter of the residential property taxes that would be paid under uniform and equal taxation is arbitrarily wiped off the tax rolls and most of the burden is shifted to other property owners.

While it is not true in every case, we can find many examples of struggling rural main street businesses and farmers subsidizing wealthy homeowners. Thus, it can be said that our property tax system contributes to the demise of main street businesses in rural communities and continued decline in farm numbers. Iowa's residential property tax rollback is but another example of providing political favors to attract votes instead of defending principles of equity, fairness, and good government.

As we consider lowering the property tax burden, special emphasis should be given to restoring the fundamental principle of uniform and equal taxation of property, even if it takes a Constitutional amendment to do so. Several states have such provisions in their state constitutions. If there are any exceptions to be made from the uniform and equal taxation principle, they should be made by a vote of the people.

In the short run, it may be politically unfeasible to eliminate the property tax rollback on residential property. It may be easier to develop a longer term plan that would bring property taxes on other forms of property down and equalize residential property over a decade.

Proposals allowing local governments to grant property tax exemptions for new machinery and equipment purchases and investment in livestock structures may be viewed as a partial counter attack by interests that have received an increasing share of property tax burden. However, this approach to economic development is divisive and ripe for building government bureaucracy and political patronage. They do not achieve uniform and equal property taxation. Similarly, the proposal for adding residential property tax credits for low income Iowans passed by the 1993 General Assembly, but vetoed by the Governor, was designed to provide preferential treatment for a favored political interest and would not achieve uniform and equal property taxation either.

If we are to lower the overall property tax burden as suggested by citizen preferences, we must shift the burden to other taxes. It is curious that Iowa's status quo politicians have avoided examining tax policy reform with the same degree of resolve and enthusiasm it has attacked government spending reform. Iowans must not suffer from the illusion that all subsidies come in the form of government spending. Many subsidies come in the form of tax subsidies, tax expenditures or tax breaks to special interests and high income citizens.

A reason tax policy reform may have been avoided up to now is that special interests and political support might be threatened. However, we cannot hope to solve our budget deficit and move our state forward in unified fashion, unless Iowans conclude that a fair and balanced approach has been used to eliminate the GAAP deficit and all cards have been laid on top of the table. If cutting funding for foster care, medicaid, and special education are on the table, then reducing tax subsidies to the wealthy for homestead credits, property tax rollbacks, food for the wealthy, "Cadillac" health care benefits, and federal income tax deductions ought to be discussed during the debate.

A 1991 report by Citizens for Tax Justice showed all state and local taxes combined represented seven percent of total income for Iowans in the highest income brackets. However, state and local taxes represented 12 percent of income for Iowans in the lowest income brackets. Middle income Iowans were at nine percent. This was before the 1992 sales tax hike, so the range between high and low income Iowans is greater now than it was then.

If we don't discuss all options, then we are only doing half of our homework and deserve half a grade. Iowa citizens will not be united if one half the state continually tries to shift the burden to the other half of the state. If this is the game we are in, we spend all of our energies figuring out who the "shiftors" and the "shiftees" will be. And, we could probably change the word from "shift" to "shaft". As a divided people, our state cannot move forward in rebuilding Iowa's jobs base for the future.

11. A Pro-Savings and Pro-Investment Tax Code.

If we are going to accomplish the economic growth goals outlined in Chapter 1, Iowa must develop a pro-savings and pro-investment tax code that will become a model for the country to follow. Status quo budget policy coupled with status quo trends in Iowa's economy and Iowa's aging population means more budget crises in decades after the year 2000. To avoid the future crises, we need to rebuild our jobs base and dramatically expand Iowa's income generating capacity. In order to do that, we need to develop one of the best pro-savings and pro-investment tax codes in the country. Striving to be 25th out of 50 will not do.

We cannot afford any more increases in our collective tax burden. These proposals are not to be misinterpreted as major tax increases. They are entirely consistent with priority two: no more tax increases. Any suggestion to the contrary should be labeled misinformation, misunderstanding, or worse. One must look at the big picture to draw the bottom line conclusions.

As outlined in Chapter 1, the three major incentives for making Iowa's tax code more pro-savings and pro-investment are tax free savings instruments, investment tax credits, and inflation adjustments on the capital gains taxes that target investment toward creating Iowa's future jobs base.

In order to adopt these three major incentives, we must hold the line on Iowa's present total collective tax burden and eliminate other tax subsidies and favors that do not reward Iowans for savings and investment in Iowa. In other words, we must stop rewarding people for buying food, borrowing to own a second home, and paying their federal taxes. Instead, we should reward them for increasing their savings and investing in enterprises that create higher-paying jobs in Iowa.

Under the new tax policy, many rich people who benefitted from the old tax subsidies will pay less in total taxes under the new system as long as they save and invest in rebuilding Iowa's jobs base. There is no question, taxes would go up for some Iowans who don't save or invest in Iowa's future. It can be argued they have already been living higher on the hog to the detriment of future generations. The approach of shifting the tax subsidies around simply recoups some of the detriment so our children can have a brighter future. Only those against more incentives for saving, investment and economic growth can oppose the merits of a pro-savings and pro-investment tax code in Iowa.

What specific tax subsidies should be traded for incentives to save and invest? One proposal is to eliminate or cap the deductibility of federal income taxes deducted on Iowa income tax returns. Opponents argue this amounts to double taxation. However this is a weak argument. Sales taxes are no longer deductible for individuals on the federal income tax return, but people haven't complained about this form of double taxation. Only when the proposed double taxation is on my return, do I get concerned about it. As a result, this argument doesn't hold water because the high income groups are also the ones who will benefit from the new savings and investment incentives in Iowa's code.

Another example is Iowa's sales tax exemptions. Iowa exempts sales taxes on food consumed at home and prescription drugs for the rich and wealthy. Several tax consultants have suggested to Iowa lawmakers that we should collect sales tax on food and prescription drugs and then provide a sales tax rebate to poor Iowans who really need it. This could be done by adding a bonus for the 180,000 food stamp recipients in Iowa and/or providing low-income tax credits on state income tax returns. Why should Iowans subsidize food and drugs for rich people?

Another subsidy for the wealthy is the tax exemption on employer-paid "Cadillac" health insurance benefits. We are now learning that not all employer-provided health care policies are the same. Some full coverage health plans have few if any deductibles and cover everything that money can conceivably buy. Such programs are purchased with tax free dollars by employers and encourage excessive health costs. Other health care plans for average people have higher deductibles and only cover catastrophic costs. Excessive employer contributions for health benefits to the wealthy should be taxed as ordinary income. Why should we subsidize the rich with "Cadillac" health care services?

In addition, Iowa provides $160 property tax relief in the form of a homestead credit for every Iowa homeowner regardless of whether its a $10,000 house or a million dollar house. A homestead credit reduces the property taxes paid by the property owner, but this is made up by increased state aid to the local units of government. Most wealthy people wouldn't miss this subsidy.

Under current income tax law, the federal government and Iowa allow homeowners to deduct interest on mortgages up to one million dollars. Why should Iowans subsidize interest on huge expensive homes? People with two homes have one as their principal residence and another one at the lake or in the mountains. If you own two homes, why should Iowans subsidize the interest on the second home? Just because it is legal for federal tax purposes does not make it the right policy for Iowa tax purposes.

Some of these ideas could be coupled with creation of community-based and industry-based Iowa Development Funds. These tax exempt funds would manage venture capital from all over Iowa increasing access and ownership in Iowa business enterprise by average citizens. With strong tax incentives and more of our own resources on the line, local citizens would provide greater support for their community's economic development. No longer would an elite few be the only ones with a piece of Iowa's pie.

12. Leadership That Listens and Leads by Example.

Many of the above ideas are rough and need refinement. Some should be tried on a pilot basis in communities ready and willing to try something different. But our guiding principle is simple: We want to reward all citizens—rich and poor—who invest their talents and resources in rebuilding Iowa's future. We would create an environment for turning the ostriches among us into forward looking entrepreneurs that are determined to leave this state in better shape for the next generation.

In the 1960s and 1970s we were led to believe more government could solve our problems. It tried. It couldn't. It made some problems worse. In the 1980s, we were led to believe the private sector could solve our problems. It tried. It couldn't. It made some problems worse. Some people became richer. A lot more became poorer. The real income earned by the average wage earner in 1992 was the same as 1986.

During the 1990s it will take all of our combined talents and resources from the public and private sectors working together and functioning as a team to rebuild our jobs base and to restore our international competitiveness.

Our two political parties have been locked into ideologies and partisan bickering, while the silent majority in our population waits for leadership to make our democracy work better and our economy to improve. Citizens want leaders who will do the right thing. Citizens want leaders who demonstrate fiscal responsibility. Citizens want leaders who defend the principles of good government and fair play. Citizens want leaders who will involve Iowans in rebuilding our job base with a balanced plan that the people of the state can discuss and support.

Chapter 3. Restoring Political Leadership.

1. Replace Hamiltonian with Jeffersonian Democracy.

Iowa citizens are frustrated with professional politicians and government. This frustration appears to be at an all time high. It stems from ethics problems, budget problems, heavy-handed decision-making processes and domineering styles of leadership. Before we can hope to reform it, we must understand what it is that bugs us. Then, we must identify the principles of democracy being violated before we can reorganize accordingly.

In 1992, the Iowa Public Policy Education Project (PPEP) organized a bi-partisan focus group of 30 respected citizens representing diverse interests from across the state. The group held five days of discussions with state leaders and experts to examine solutions for solving the Iowa budget crisis. During the informal discussion, the group identified examples from recent years where Iowa's style of leadership departed from what was believed to be fundamental democratic principles. These points are adapted from a column I wrote for the *Des Moines Register* on July 28, 1992.

(1) Major public policy decisions appear to be made by a few power elite with little public discourse. In some cases, broad citizen involvement from across Iowa appears to be limited or excluded from discussions on major new policy initiatives, government organization, and service delivery. Examples include passing the fiber optics network without surveys of local interest and the Spending Reform Commission's call for massive local government consolidation without significant local input.

(2) Public information on the economy and evaluations of public institutions appear to be controlled, limited and sometimes distorted by political professionals. When citizens do not have access to fact-based evidence on public issues and government performance, they are left to make their decisions based on myths, emotionalism, and propaganda.

(3) Special interest political concerns have taken priority over enlightened public interests. Powerful and elite

interests have formed statewide "democratic-like education programs and leadership coalitions" designed more to promote discussion of favorite solutions and generate support rather than to inform citizens about the facts and alternatives.

(4) In both parties, personal aspirations, partisan concerns and loyalty to party leadership have been given priority over ethics, performance in government and doing right for Iowans. In some cases, party actives continue to chastise those who have fulfilled their constitutional duties and who have publicly raised concerns about the ethics and/or fiscal responsibility of political superiors.

For example, the State Auditor was attacked by party actives for fulfilling his constitutional duties and publicly questioning Iowa's creative budgeting practices. The firing of a Deputy State Treasurer was linked to her attempts to warn federal and state officials about potential problems with Iowa Trust a year before the scandal was publicly revealed.

(5) The principles of sound fiscal management in the state budget appear to have been ignored. After a decade of "fudge and spend" fiscal policy, it may take several years to restore fiscal responsibility and citizen confidence in government.

(6) The use of "good" management principles appears to be inadequate to generate high quality performance among public employees within some state and local government institutions. One cannot encourage Total Quality Management principles in the public sector on one hand and bring suit against public employees and ignore local government concerns on the other.

The debate over the style of leadership appropriate for government is not new. In fact, perhaps the most classic debate in our nation's history occurred between Alexander Hamilton and Thomas Jefferson during the framing of our national Constitution. The essence of the debate fits Iowa today as we analyze the decision processes that have contributed to citizen frustrations of the past decade and the style of leadership that will move the state forward in the future.

One might paraphrase the Hamiltonian philosophy by saying that he loved the citizens of this country so much that he believed the enlightened elite should make policy decisions on behalf of the citizens, so that their best interests could be provided for in government policy. In other words, Hamilton favored a strong central government in which most of the decisions and debate would be conducted by enlightened interests and representatives based on their view of the world.

In contrast, Jefferson said, "I know of no safe depository of the ultimate powers of society but the people themselves; and if we think the people are not enlightened enough to exercise their power with wholesome discretion, the remedy is not to take the decision-making power from them, but to inform their discretion." Jefferson was clearly more of a progressive populist who believed that the people would contribute to solving their own problems if they understood the issues and were involved in making the decisions.

Focus groups and other discussions across the state indicate that Iowans are opposed to throwing out our democracy. However, many are ready to replace our Hamiltonian approach with a Jeffersonian approach to democracy. How would it compare or contrast with the recent Iowa examples outlined?

(1) Iowa's political leadership would support and reward efforts to engage the broadest range of citizen interests in TV town meetings, issue study groups and citizen discussions as a regular part of the budget and policy decision-making process.

(2) Iowa's political leadership would conduct and reward efforts to increase the amount of policy-relevant information available to citizens. It would reward efforts to provide vital accountability information regarding the performance of state and local government institutions. Citizen understanding doesn't happen by accident. It takes resources, balanced and objective information, and deliberate efforts to achieve accountability as perceived by the citizenry.

(3) Iowa citizens and Iowa's leadership would reward actions that demonstrate statesmanship and public interest above special interests, partisan loyalty, and personal aspirations.

(4) Iowa citizens and Iowa's leadership would reward efforts to expose breeches of ethics and to protect the integrity of our government over partisan loyalty or personal opportunity.

(5) Iowa's leadership would conduct and reward efforts to pursue sound fiscal management and promote greater performance of our government institutions.

(6) Iowa's leadership would conduct and reward efforts demonstrating principles of good management, innovation, efficiency, and high performance in serving the public.

2. Citizen Voter Initiative Process.

Iowans could solve many of the recent abuses of Jeffersonian principles by adopting a voter initiative process. Citizens need a tool to send a message to the professional politicians and Hamiltonian elite that there will not be business as usual in the future. We can do that by rebalancing the powers among the citizenry and politicians in Iowa's Constitution.

Voter initiative processes give citizens the right to (1) complete a petition process for placing any previously passed law on the ballot for voter approval or rejection, (2) complete a petition process to place any voter initiated bill on the ballot for passage into law or rejection, and (3) to approve or reject resolutions initiated by voter petition or referred by both houses of the legislature. With safeguards to limit initiatives to major policy issues and to limit voting to general elections, popular vote would represent a major step toward increasing citizen participation and reducing the frustrations that exist.

Legislators and governors would think twice about certain policies if they knew voters could overturn bad ideas which don't have broad public support. Any proposal rammed through the legislative process—like the fiber optics—could be challenged. Politicians would spend less time pandering to special interests and more time discussing issues and educating constituents.

Voter initiatives would strengthen the Jeffersonian principle that the informed collective choice of the many results in better public policy than the public choices made by an elite few. In this case, we are not talking about taking decision-making power away from the professional politicians and corporate elite. But, voter initiative would provide another check and balance consistent with the Constitutional principle that the people retain supreme political power in our democracy.

Many fears about potential problems are overblown. Yes, there may be a correlation between dollars spent and the outcomes of voter initiatives. However, this argument is not a sufficient reason for not having a voter initiative process. Does the correlation between dollars spent lobbying and legislative outcomes under our present system mean that we shouldn't have a legislature? No, it simply means some safeguards are needed.

I have worked in states with the voter initiative process and I'm aware of examples where the citizens have regularly voted against the side that was better financed. The important factor is whether citizens have access to the facts and balanced, nonpartisan citizen education programs that objectively examine the alternatives and consequences. In addition, processes can be developed to limit the number of initiatives and to assure the citizenry that the most important questions are on the ballot.

The bottom line is that citizen understanding and involvement increases to make our democracy stronger. Voter initiative processes force us to do our homework, use our heads, and take responsibility for our democracy. More citizens will take their responsibility seriously and many will seek out the facts and information. Citizens in Iowa would have another avenue of influence and control over the public decision-making process. Iowans would be better able to voice their collective views on priority issues and potential abuses of political power.

Finally, Iowa lawmakers have increasingly encouraged the use of local referendums by giving citizens increased responsibility in setting local policy. The local referendums are seen as an important step in strengthening local government by giving more citizen power to create a check and balance against local officials. It only seems logical that a similar state-level process would be useful in strengthening citizen responsibility and providing an additional check and balance in state policy.

3. Term Limits for the Chief Executive.

Our founders considered length of term to be among the fundamental characteristics distinguishing democracy from the systems of tyranny that characterized the monarchies of Europe. Of particular concern were the potential abuses of power that could occur when a single ruler served for life.

A chief argument for term limits on the Office of Governor is that the chief executive holds power over three branches of government. He or she holds appointment and administrative powers over the executive branch, appointment powers over the judicial branch, and veto power over the legislature.

There is increasing opportunity for abuses of power as political partisans become more entrenched in agency positions, state boards, commissions, and court benches. Potential abuses of executive power appear after a period of years when the same people, interests, and philosophies are reappointed. Instead of having a government of the people, by the people, and for the people, we end up with a government more loyal to serving and protecting the leadership and their jobs. Our system of checks and balances erodes.

While term limits were not initially written into the U.S. Constitution, by gentleman's agreement Presidents Washington, Adams, and Jefferson established a tradition in which the chief executive did not run for President for more than two terms. This tradition continued until President Franklin D. Roosevelt was elected for four terms during the Great Depression and World War II. After President Roosevelt, our nation and states passed the 22nd Amendment to the U.S. Constitution which limited all future Presidents to two terms.

Today, 40 states have term limits for their Governors. Iowa is one of only ten states without term limits for the chief executive. One state sets the limit at three four-year terms. Thirty-six states set limits at eight years or two-four year terms. Three states have even set limits to serving one four-year term without succession.

Recently, several states have also passed term limits for state and federal offices by referendum during the 1992 elections. Fifteen states passed term limits on state legislative and executive offices and 15 states passed term limits on their respective U.S. Senate and Congressional Representatives. However, clearly the greatest number of term limit policies of the 50 states are imposed on chief executives.

Many citizens feel that we have begun to see the symptoms that can result from lack of term limits in Iowa.

Partisan interests increasingly overshadow public interests and interests of the citizens. Executive proposals for the legislature to meet every other year appear as attempts to consolidate executive power. Loyalty to party leadership can eventually become more important than defending the Constitution and serving citizens.

As an example, issues relating to the composition of the Iowa Board of Regents have been widely reported during the past two years. In 1992, five of the nine regents were alumni of the University of Iowa, two were alumni of the University of Northern Iowa, and none were Iowa State alumni.

In addition, seven of nine Regents represented the 13 most urban counties in Iowa with half of Iowa's population. However, the 86 least populated counties with the other half of Iowa's population were represented by only two Regents. In proportion to population, Polk County should have one Regent, but has had two. The Governor's initial nominees for 1993 would have reduced the urban/rural resident bias to a six to three voting margin, but would have retained two Regents from Polk County. After the rejection of one Polk County nominee, the Governor appointed a Cedar Rapids attorney, therefore the urban voting margin remained the same.

It is with great interest that such a board dominated by urban alumni of two schools would force the sale of a major asset of the third over the wishes of its president, faculty senate, students and alumni. Perhaps even more important, the Regent alumni of the two schools appear to have interpreted the mission of the third to be much narrower than what currently exists or than what is favored by the stakeholders of the third university.

Furthermore, the former chairman of the Regents sat on the Board of the major private university in Des Moines. He was a major fund raiser for the Governor's political campaigns. This injects an aura of politics and potential conflict of interests into higher education policy-making and management. The Governor, also an alum of two other Iowa universities, sided with the Regents by vetoing legislation blocking the WOI-TV sale.

Iowa citizens would not normally suspect school rivalry to be a factor in such decisions. Citizens normally expect the Regents and Governor to make impartial policy decisions after hearing input from all affected interests in the state. However, it was widely reported that several respected Iowa citizens were treated poorly during the Regent hearing process.

While the intentions of the Governor and the Regents may be completely honorable, the facts provide an appearance of the potential favoritism and bias in the decision-making process. This appearance could have been completely avoided if basic democratic principles had been followed in making balanced appointments to the Regents. Before you conclude that I may have my own bias with respect to the Regents, let me say that this is only one of several boards and commissions where problems have developed because of special interest appointments. Other examples are cited throughout the remainder of the book.

Citizens need to be able to take pride in their democracy. We need faith that our policy decisions will be reviewed by balanced boards that will consider all of the relevant positions and interests. We need faith that our administrative decisions will be based on the best impartial judgment of Iowa's public interest. Democracy should create an atmosphere where all citizens are free to speak without fear of retaliation. Only then, can there be confidence that the best ideas have been put on the table and that judgments have been made in the best interests of the state, instead of elite special interests.

Today, not all Iowans have faith that the relevant views are being presented and carefully considered. Faith and pride must be restored if we are to move Iowa forward. If two terms are good enough for the President to redirect the course of this nation and accomplish the will of the people, the same is surely true for the governor of a state.

If citizens desire the present philosophy be continued in office, then it is the duty and responsibility of the parties to develop new leaders who can carry on that philosophy and provide new ideas for the future. Term limits on the chief executive and possibly for Legislative and Congressional offices would be a step toward strengthening democratic principles in Iowa and reassuring Iowans that our future is not limited by a narrow set of elite interests possessing fund raising capability.

4. Judicious, Independent and Balanced Commissions.

Several members of the Governor's Commission on Spending Reform are to be respected for their accomplishments. The Commission did a credible job in suggesting ways to improve the budgetary process for restoring Iowa's fiscal responsibility. There is some logic in having "hard nosed" private sector corporate fiscal conservatives suggest improvements in the budget process. After all, they are familiar with budget controls and auditing processes required to keep large corporations afloat.

On the other hand, a narrowly defined commission dominated by urban corporate executives is not the group to restructure rural local government, to examine tax subsidies, to set spending priorities or to protect the diverse interests of Iowa citizens. For examining those issues, Iowans should have had a more diverse commission that aggressively sought input from citizens whose interests were at stake. The way in which the Commission was appointed almost guaranteed that only limited success would be achieved in government spending priorities and structural reform.

The charge given to the Commission was limited to spending reform and government efficiency. But, efficiency is not the only criterion for examining the performance of government. If it were, we would not have a democracy, because democracy is not the most efficient form of government. Democratic processes require time for public debate, examination of alternative solutions, extra rules to assure fair play, and checks and balances within the political decision-making and implementation processes. Philosophers argue that dictatorships and military juntas are probably more efficient than democracies, but who among us wants a dictatorship? Most of us would prefer control retained by the people and accountability provided by democracy.

Of the 22 members of the Governor's Commission, nine came from Polk County. Polk County accounts for 12 percent of Iowa's population. So in proportion to population, Polk County should have had only three representatives.

The state's 13 largest counties possess half of Iowa's population, but accounted for 19 of 22 Commission members. The remaining 86 counties representing all of Iowa's rural counties also contain 50 percent of the Iowa's total population, but they had only three representatives on the Commission.

The southern three tiers of counties possess 20 percent of Iowa's population, but had one representative instead of four. The northern two tier of counties have 12 percent of Iowa's population but only had one representative instead of three.

To make matters worse, much of the work in developing recommendations came from seven task forces that were dominated by Polk County residents. Sixty-seven task force members resided in Polk County, while only 40 came from outside of Polk County.

Yes, it is true that the task forces were designed to include state officials and state government expertise. And, it is true that a few lobbyists on the task forces and Commission represented rural interests even though they resided in Polk County. However, it was publicly reported that task forces used voice vote to move recommendations forward for consideration by the full Commission.

Since Polk County possessed three votes to every two for the remaining counties in the state, which proposals do you suppose moved forward? It is not surprising that many rural non-Polk County residents felt left out of the process. Such processes violate Jeffersonian principles. In a democracy, the means are often as important as the ends. The one-person-one-vote principle was violated in the method of making appointments to both the Commission and its task forces.

Members of the Governor's Commission on Spending Reform are not without special interests of their own. A few months after the CEO of Younkers publicly called for reducing the number of school districts from 438 to 125, his firm was threatening to move corporate jobs from Iowa to Wisconsin unless subsidies and grants from Wisconsin were matched. So we had a private firm cutting government spending on one hand and requesting government subsidies on the other. The *Des Moines Register* later disclosed Wisconsin never pledged any subsidies. The Younkers chief retracted his request. Recently, Younkers continued to attract controversy over government incentives.

In other matters, the Governor's Commission tackled county government consolidation without a great degree of familiarity with the institutions they were assessing. On the other hand, the Commission conducted a limited examination of the single largest new statewide investment in fiber optics, for which the Commission would seemingly have more expertise. The Commission claimed the fiber optics network was a done deal and the only option under consideration was whether or not to privatize it. Since then, however, the media has reported state officials rushed the construction contracts to prevent strong examination by the Commission on Spending Reform.

In the final analysis, the Commission on Spending Reform has had a positive impact on the budget process and Iowans can take a measure of pride in this effort. However, we should not conclude the Governor's Commission was even-handed on all issues or that their analysis was accurate and realistic in all areas. Control was not balanced among rural and urban interests. The interests of many Iowans may not have been given fair consideration when the Commission moved beyond budget process issues.

During the last state government reorganization in 1987, numerous independent boards and commissions were disbanded from riding herd over the various agencies of state government. However, only a few years later, the Administration has come to rely on quasi-independent commissions to improve state budget processes and health care reform. Apparently, the value of having commissions somewhat independent of the political process has been rediscovered to possess merit. However, if Iowa is again to make more use of independent boards and commissions, we must assure they are not elitist in terms of the interests represented. They should be representative of Iowa's diverse citizen interests and they should be able to operate with appropriate discretion.

In the corporate world, external auditors normally operate independently of the CEO and the CEO's management team. In most cases, external auditors report directly to the Board of Directors. This is done to limit the potential influence from the CEO, so that any potential problems with management can be uncovered. If we view the people of Iowa as the Board of Directors and stockholders of the State of Iowa, citizens are entitled to get an audit of Iowa's budget processes and programs independent of the direct span of control of the Chief Executive.

Perhaps the Commission on Spending Reform should have been appointed in a manner that would have allowed it to work independently of the Governor and more closely with the State Auditor. In contrast, however, when the State Auditor fulfilled his constitutional responsibilities and revealed accounting irregularities that contributed to the GAAP deficit, the Administration responded by proposing to cut the budget for the State Auditor's Office by 25 percent. Iowans should oppose this kind of behavior if we want fiscal responsibility. As a matter of principle, the Auditor's budget should be increased during times of apparent fiscal mismanagement.

Iowa should restore the judicious use of independent, bi-partisan, and balanced boards and commissions, particularly in areas like ethics, campaign finance, spending reforms, tax subsidy reforms, government structure and organization, and health care. These are areas where the potential abuses of political power are great and we cannot legislate every detail that will come up. These are the areas in which Iowa citizens now need greater powers of oversight if we wish to restore the principles of good government and Jeffersonian democracy.

5. Citizen Confidence Requires Higher Ethics.

Iowans watched another example in 1992. Our status quo political process was very awkward in responding to alleged ethics violations of former Senate President Joe Welsh relating to the Iowa Trust scandal. Many Iowa citizens are now skeptical about whether a majority party would discipline their own leaders in a fashion similar to minority party members or similar to the average citizen. Most of us were brought up to respect the concepts of equal justice, rule of law, and separation of powers.

Several events during the handling of the Welsh investigation have led average citizens to wonder whether equal justice and rule of law exist in Iowa's political institutions. During the investigation, there was the potential appearance of placing party loyalty above impartial consideration of the facts. An independent ethics commission would have provided a forum that would have been perceived as more impartial by average citizens.

In fact, a bi-partisan independent commission of prominent Iowa citizens was appointed during the Welsh hearings to study ethics reform during 1992. This commission recommended that a permanent bi-partisan independent ethics commission be set up to provide an impartial forum for reviewing alleged ethics violations by legislators, lobbyists, and other state officials.

However, to date, the Iowa Senate has opposed and prevented the passage of the independent citizen ethics commission proposal. The Iowa Senate is the very body that publicly appeared to mishandle the Welsh investigation process. It appears that some policymakers don't want citizens judging their conduct. Such attitudes are unacceptable in the minds of many citizens. If the Senate does not get the message, perhaps the independent ethics commission should become one of the first initiative proposals to be considered by voters.

In the absence of an independent commission, one might think that the judicial branch of government should have presided over the alleged violations. This approach could have provided a more impartial setting for examining alleged violations of the ethics laws. However, attempts to move the investigation to the legal system were effectively stopped by the Attorney General's Office, which refused to examine the allegations against Welsh claiming that it was the responsibility of the Polk County Attorney.

The Attorney General's Office could have avoided the appearance of partisan politics by calling for or spearheading an independent investigation regarding Iowa law on official misconduct or other more serious charges and/or calling for a Grand Jury of citizens to issue an indictment or to vindicate those involved .

The Attorney General officially is the Chief of our Department of Justice and according to statutes has the authority to become involved "when, in the Attorney General's judgment, the interest of the state requires such action." Citizens may find it curious that an Attorney General's Office would relegate a major investigation potentially involving a crisis in the state's political processes to a local County Attorney. While this represents standard procedure for most cases, it represents a minimum effort for a case with statewide interest and impact. From the number of speeches and press releases on various crimes that have appeared in local papers across Iowa, it would appear the Attorney General's Office has great latitude to investigate whatever issues it sees fit, and often does so if the issue is perceived to violate Iowa's laws.

While there may not be proof that partisan politics or personal aspirations influenced the decisions, there is an appearance of circumstantial evidence for this potential to have occured. The Attorney General has expressed gubernatorial aspirations and formerly served as the State Chair of the Democratic Party. The Democrats were the majority party in the Senate and Welsh was a Democrat. As a result, regular citizens who read between the lines are given room for doubt about whether equal justice is uniformly applied to politicians in Iowa.

The bottom line is that the Attorney General chose the path of minimum response and missed another golden opportunity to demonstrate that the Attorney General's Office provides strong leadership on ethics in government, that no politician is above the law, and that equal justice and rule of law is placed above partisan politics and personal aspirations. As a result, Iowans will now wonder if they can count on having the interests of Iowa and its citizens put above partisan interests when it comes to other tough decisions in a crisis.

After awhile citizens start to question whether this is what happens when politicians begin to view politics as a professional career. People wonder whether party position and support become more important than protecting the fundamental principles of democracy. Judicious use of independent, bipartisan and balanced commissions and boards would help to take back some control from the professional politicians. It would provide another way for the people of Iowa to restore our democracy and to make sure that our political process does what is right with respect to democratic principles and its citizens.

6. Campaign and Lobbying Reforms Favoring Constituents.

The most important action we can take to strengthen our democracy is to vote and to treat our elections seriously. Candidates must be required to lay out their proposed solutions to the problems that confront us. Many professional politicians avoid straight talk. They prefer to stick with safe themes and rhetoric that appeal to the voters' self interests without laying all their cards on the table.

In future elections, Iowans cannot allow candidates to ignore our state's economic performance and budget deficit. If one candidate talks about building new prisons, ask her where the money is coming from and what the constitutional limits on debt really mean? If the other candidate talks about four more years to finish the job he started, ask him why he hasn't been able to get the job done by now? Why would four more years be any different? If we hold the candidates more accountable, we will solve many of the problems we face in Iowa's democracy. We will have completed part of our responsibility as citizens, regardless of whom we may vote for.

If we are unhappy or dissatisfied with the responses, in the words of Ross Perot, we must "throw the rascals out." That is the way our democratic process works. Iowa citizens sent a message to the statehouse during the last legislative session. The Republicans are now in control of the House and they made some gains in the Senate. In return, the new Republican majority sent a strong message early in the 1993 General Assembly, when they demonstrated they were willing to put fiscal responsibility above other interests. They were willing to consider a stronger measure of fiscal responsibility than the Administration or Senate demonstrated.

Changing leadership alone won't restore Iowa's democracy. But it may stimulate reform. There is a tendency for people in the system to stay there too long. Having some members in the legislature with a measure of experience is good, but those who stay there too long become encrusted in the system. They get used to the same perks and procedures as those who were there before.

In a sense, the aristocracy driven out during our Revolution has been replaced with our own version: a political nobility that is sometimes immune to the people's will. Created through campaign and lobbying laws and lack of term limits, we have a series of incentives that give the edge to special interests who contribute to campaigns and in turn to incumbents who do the right thing for their campaign contributors. This is not only a national concern, but is a concern in Iowa as well.

Lobbyists notice that legislators are more likely to return phone calls if their Political Action Committees (PAC) have given money. Whom are we kidding? We know what is being bought. We are told that campaign contributions provide access. We also know that all interests are after a favorable vote and favorable policy for their special interest. When those who profit from the policy decisions turn out to be big campaign contributors, we have to be naive to believe there is no connection.

In school, we learned that tyranny meant abuse of power. It usually occurred in small tropical Republics, not in our democracy. Well! Here we are Iowans, some issues contrary to positions of the state's most powerful interests cannot be presented publicly without an expectation that 153 letters will be sent to policymakers and the media attacking the presenter's credibility and character. As usual, the bad apples overshadow exemplary behavior of many other policymakers and lobbyists. But it happened in 1993 in Iowa.

Today, we hear more polite references to conflicts of interest or alleged ethics problems. But why else would individuals and PACs representing special interests account for most of the financing of political campaigns? If average citizens are to matter to the politicians, we the people must figure out ways for our campaign finance laws to give the edge in control to regular people who are the legislator's constituents.

A national scientific survey of 1,733 adults conducted by the Gordon S. Black Corporation in March 1993 after a Ross Perot town meeting indicated that 70 percent of the respondents would pass new laws that would eliminate all possibility of special interests giving large sums of money to candidates. Seventy-eight percent would reduce domestic lobbying to the giving of information only. Sixty-nine percent would eliminate Political Action Committees and their campaign contributions. These are fairly high numbers by most standards.

We need an independent campaign commission with greater powers to investigate unethical conduct and present findings to voters prior to elections. All firms doing business with the state should be prohibited from making political contributions to those directly responsible for passing legislation and regulating their industry. We need a different way for such contributions to be made without an apparent direct conflict of interest.

All campaign contributions to candidates from people and PACs other than resident constituents should be limited to $1,000. Out-of-state PACs and interests should not be allowed to contribute at all. The direct contributions from Iowa Political Action Committees should be reduced. We should change the rules so most of a candidate's contributions comes from local constituents instead of outsiders. And, voters should be made aware of who the largest contributors are by publishing a list of the top names in local papers prior to each election.

Finally, some of our elected and appointed officials may see their terms of office as an interim step to a higher paying lobbying job. Recently, a former House Speaker and gubernatorial candidate became a lobbyist. A former Senate Minority Leader became a lobbyist. A former Senate Majority Leader and gubernatorial candidate became a lobbyist. The Governor's former Chief of Staff joined a law firm to counsel clients with an interest in state government spending.

In a couple of cases, not only did they cash in on their experience but they earned income on projects they previously helped to pass—fiber optics being one case in point. To prevent such actions in the future, Iowans should prohibit anyone who has held any political position in the government from directly profiting from policy decisions for which they made or influenced in official capacity. We need an independent citizens' ethics commission with clout to ride herd on such behavior.

7. Engaging Citizens in the Process.

Owners have responsibilities, too. One of the best ideas coming from Iowa citizen leaders involved in a recent PPEP Focus Group was a new way of involving citizens in the budget process. Legislative leadership knows that some unacceptable proposals can be rammed through the appropriations process during the last hours of the legislative session. Why not require the budget to be passed by a certain deadline and then temporarily adjourn the legislature for two weeks to hold field hearings and statewide TV broadcasts on the budget before making final decisions?

Such a process would serve to give the Fiscal Bureau time to finish all of the fiscal notes on estimated costs and it would give all elected legislators and citizens adequate time to read the fine print in the budget. It would provide an opportunity to inform a cross-section of citizens across the state on the budget priorities and compromises to gauge reaction. And it would provide an opportunity to make any necessary final adjustments.

If Iowa citizens are to bear some of the responsibility for Iowa's budget crisis, it is because we did not insist on accurate, objective and independent information on the status of our budget during the past decade. If we allow the present system to continue unreformed, then we the people of Iowa will bear more responsibility for the next budget crisis.

Citizens need greater access to relevant information. We need regular disclosure of Iowa's budget status. We deserve independent audits. Time and resources are needed to involve community leaders and citizens from across the state in setting priorities. We must encourage, teach and ask regular citizens to become involved in our political process.

A recent national study by the Kettering Foundation concluded that citizens want to participate in the political events, processes, activities and educational forums on public issues, but they are constrained by political institutions, special interests, limited locations, and/or out-of-pocket costs of transportation and time. We must recognize that our citizens are working longer hours and frequently both parents are working. Therefore, we have to work harder in providing citizens with access so they can perform their responsibilities. If we don't, our democracy will continue to be weak and Iowa's political leadership can continue to behave as in the past.

For example, Iowa has done pioneering work with statewide TV town meetings and focus groups on public issues. The effort won statewide and national recognition. Iowa was doing interactive "electronic town hall" meetings three years before the idea gained national recognition in the last Presidential election.

Such approaches have been shown to be more cost-efficient and demonstrate greater educational impact in comparison traditional adult education program delivery. While some Iowa TV stations have collaborated on additional specials, Iowa citizens would greatly benefit from a regular series of two to four balanced and objective statewide TV town meetings on priority issues each year. Future programs should also be more balanced in providing citizens information and providing citizens with an opportunity to present their questions, views, and comments.

In summary Iowa citizens must also bear some of the responsibility for events of the past decade. We have ignored our responsibilities as owners of Iowa. Our political system can only be repaired if we take charge of it. We can only take charge of it, if we understand the political process and the priority issues we face.

New institutions must be invented to return more authority over our government to Iowa citizens. Iowans must have the ability to watch and monitor our politicians and political process more closely so we know they are doing the right things and sticking to democratic principles. It is our responsibility. It is the only way citizens will regain confidence in our government. If we don't, the other actions we take in repairing our budget deficit and economy will likely represent a temporary fix.

We need more decisions by leaders who visit with the people and aggressively gather citizen input. We need leaders who weigh citizen input and make decisions that reflect what is best for Iowa's future. The decisions must be plain and clear. Citizens must be given reasonable justification so they can understand, support, and help implement the policy decisions and priorities.

Government is not a candy store for every group to pick up any jar it wants. This is not free money. It is our money. More importantly, it may be our children's money. We must tackle the problems now like our parents and grandparents would have done. Let's fix it and keep it fixed so our children and grandchildren remember us with pride as they take responsibility for their democracy and recall the actions of our generation.

Chapter 4. Reinventing Local Government.

1. Myth: Consolidation Reduces Deficits.

One of the blind alleys that Iowans have been led down in recent years is the idea that we could solve our budget crisis if we would just reorganize state government or if we would just consolidate all of those inefficient local governments across the state. This issue was fueled by flimsy anecdotal evidence and it has created major divisions between urban and rural Iowa that have impeded our ability to work together on real solutions for solving the deficit and for strengthening our economy.

Urban folks look at declining population in rural counties and the higher state aid per capita going to some rural counties. Then they say, "We urban folks are paying more than our share for government while those rural folks aren't. If they would just consolidate all those inefficient counties and small school districts, our budget problems would be cured."

In rural areas, the community leaders point to the sales tax leakage rural citizens are paying to subsidize the urban folks. Then rural folks say, "We are paying more than our share for government and those urban folks aren't. We invested a lot of money to educate our kids and they end up working in the city. So, urban folks reap the income generating capacity and returns from our rural investments. We're certainly not going to let urban folks dictate to us how we are going to organize our rural communities."

One can see that these arguments all have a thread of validity, yet they all miss the point. Few rural community leaders and citizens would disagree that their communities are going to look a lot different 30 to 50 years from now. Few would disagree that they need to plan for coming adjustments in their community institutions.

However, urban leaders and citizens should not presume all rural communities are declining or that structural change should be forced. First, consolidation does not make economic sense in all cases. Second, forcing mandatory consolidation often is a sure fire way to guarantee failure. When one set of interests imposes a policy on another against their will, you have a fight on your hands. Third, any budget efficiency savings from consolidation will not be large enough to materially affect the taxes of urban people or solve Iowa's current budget crisis.

In fact, a massive statewide restructuring effort would likely worsen the present budget deficit in the short run. Why? It is naive to believe Iowa could magically consolidate all schools and counties instantly. Institutional restructuring always requires complex feasibility studies and negotiations. The transition costs to implement consolidation can be significant. The time required for feasibility studies and negotiations would likely be six months to a year or longer and the implementation of the actual consolidation of people and functions would likely take another six months to a year before full completion.

Consolidation of most public institutions presently requires a public vote, which means developing a campaign and educational process to inform the citizens. Finally, the consolidation study, decisions, and implementation process must be done in a manner that respects the rights and interests of citizens in each community and the rest of the state.

2. Separating the Myth from Reality.

The Governor's Commission on Spending Reform made several specific local government consolidation recommendations. Iowa's county driver's licensing stations would be merged into 19 regional stations. Similar suggestions were made for merging Iowa's 99 counties into 14 to 30 regional sub-state government units. Regarding school districts, the Commission initially recommended reducing Iowa's 438 school districts to 125. Later after the firestorm, this recommendation was revised to requiring districts to increase their pupil/teacher ratios from 15 to 20. The idea was to encourage consolidation without picking a number.

The Governor's Commission on Spending Reform hired a nationally recognized business consultant who claimed that we could achieve 14 percent savings every time we double the population served. One might ask whether the estimates of savings were based on real numbers from local government consolidations or was it the same propaganda that business consultants were telling clients during the merger mania of the 1980s. That fiasco resulted in golden parachutes to CEOs and left many consolidated firms in high debt positions.

As a member of the Board of Directors for a Fortune 500 company during the 1980s, I learned that almost every merger consultant hired automatically said 10 to 20 percent savings could be achieved regardless of the nature of the entities being consolidated. That's what they were paid for. I later found such statements were often made without real hard numbers or an acknowledgment of the cost and complexity of the transition.

Complete documentation does not exist on the success or failure rate of merger studies and whether the estimated savings were ever actually achieved in the private sector. Often after mergers take place, the CEOs don't feel the need for information on whether the savings were achieved or not. Such information may show a poor decision was made, and it can't be undone. Only, if the savings were actually achieved, is it generally shared with others. Even then, information on private sector mergers does not directly apply to public sector institutions.

My point is that one could have guessed that Iowa's CEOs, like our nation's CEOs, rarely stand up to proclaim anything other than "bigger is always better." Rural community leaders and citizens have the most to gain or lose from rural consolidation. They pay most of the bill for their services. Their livelihood and personal investments are in their communities. They would pay most of the increased costs or gain the benefits from the savings that result from consolidation. Maybe they should have been fully represented on the discussions of consolidations regarding rural institutions.

The consolidation agenda seems to permeate Des Moines corporate culture clubs. According to recent rhetoric, rural Iowans should watch the decisions already being made by corporate businesses with interests in Iowa. In January 1993, a *Des Moines Register* columnist wrote, "Bring the corporate planners and their bosses in and ask them to share the thinking that is going on into the Iowa they are inventing. My guess is that the result will be 14 or so commercial centers."

Well, let's check the facts. The statements are probably true if one is listening to selected executives in Des Moines. Younkers for example just happens to have stores in 14 counties around the state. They've been pulling out of smaller Iowa communities and moving to metro centers like Omaha and Milwaukee.

But how about Wal-mart, which happens to be the largest and most successful retail corporation in the nation? They seem to think 43 Iowa counties are worth the investment. Add K-Mart, Target, and Sears to the map and it appears 51 counties are worth saving if we watch the Iowa corporate America is creating.

This reminds me of another story about a university study done 20 years ago. It concluded that since we have the technology to do so, we could have a much more efficient farm sector if we organized all of the farms into 2000 acre units. However, no one bothered to ask the 80 percent of the farmers required to quit farming what they would do or why they would sell out.

It used to be that only we ivory tower academics came up with such useless information. It now appears corporate executives and their consultants sometimes suffer from ivory tower disease too. Before we get steam-rolled, one should not always presume that the analysis and conclusions by high paid consultants are correct. Sometimes they say what the funders want to hear.

More recently, we've discovered that 2000 acre Russian collectives are not necessarily more efficient than smaller American farms. If we move from 99 counties to 14 sub-state units of government in Iowa, we would likely find that the regional governments covering three to eight counties are not always more efficient either. Consolidation and volume do not necessarily equal efficiency, quality and low cost service.

In western Kansas, Nebraska, and the Dakotas, there are still county governments in counties with less than 1000 population. Even they have not consolidated these counties. The lowest county population in Iowa is 4,866 people. Yes, some sparsely populated counties in the Great Plains are efficiently sharing services across county boundaries. But, they have not merged geographically.

3. Does Bigger Mean More Cost Efficient?

The Governor's Commission estimated that consolidating 99 counties into 14 to 30 sub-state units of government would generate $27 to $34 million in savings.

How did the Commission arrive at these estimates? The consultant simply assumed elimination of 69 to 85 counties and their respective county attorneys, auditors, engineers, recorders, sheriffs, treasurers and supervisors. The salaries and benefits were totaled and the consultant called it "efficiency savings" from consolidation. This would mean that work previously done by the above 1,353 local officials would now be done by as few as 190 remaining local officials without any increase in staff or additional pay. It certainly could be called a visionary and futuristic approach. But, it is unrealistic in terms of what can actually be achieved.

The Commission's Report shows average administrative costs per citizen reaches an optimum size at about 50,000 people. Average administrative costs at this optimum size is $28 per citizen. However, it appears that counties with a wide range of populations can exceed this optimum average cost level. The Commission's Report shows that many Iowa counties with 12,000 to 150,000 people have administrative costs below $28 per citizen. In fact, many counties with 12,000 people come close to having the lowest administrative costs in the state at $23 per capita.

Therefore, we cannot simply conclude that increasing the population served will automatically increase administrative efficiency. Counties in the range of 12,000 to 20,000 people can achieve almost all of the cost efficiency that larger counties can. So, "bigger is not necessarily always better" as far as county administration efficiency goes.

Let's take the Commission's optimum size assertion one step further. As earlier stated, the optimum county size appears to be about 50,000 people. At this size, county administrative costs average $28 per citizen. If we follow the Commission's logic, all counties ought to be reorganized to achieve the greatest efficiency. The chart shows the county administrative cost in Polk county is about $40 per person. So, according to the Commission's economies of size logic, Polk County could save $12 per citizen or $4 million in total savings by reorganizing into seven smaller more efficient counties.

This would be great, if achieving efficiency was that simple. But, it is not. Making big counties into medium size counties does not necessarily achieve efficiency for the citizens any more than making small counties into medium sized counties.

In 1988, I served as a consultant to the Iowa Department of Education and Iowa Interim Legislative School Finance Study Committee. In that role, I conducted economies of size studies on Iowa schools. Based on this experience and preliminary visual observation of the Commission's economies of size chart, it appears that only 15 of Iowa's smallest counties would likely achieve enough efficiency to generate significant cost savings from consolidation. Administrative costs in these counties are presently in the range of $40 to $80 dollars per citizen.

Even then, the combined savings from consolidating these 15 counties would likely be $3 million statewide— not $27 to $34 million as suggested by the Commission. My estimate is based on the judgment that consolidation would bring administrative costs down by $20 per citizen for the 150,000 people in the 15 counties with the highest administrative costs per citizen. In other Iowa counties, the savings per person would be smaller and the increased transportation and access costs would likely be greater than the consolidation savings.

Precise estimates are not available. This would require an actual consolidation feasibility study for the counties involved. And even then, local residents might decide they prefer to pay an extra $20, $30 or $40 per person in order to retain local services, local control and accountability.

My assessment of economies of size in Iowa local government is consistent with several other studies done in other states. A review shows there is little if any economies of size for many labor intensive functions of local government like fire, police and trash collection services. Other functions of local government can be provided more efficiently in larger population units. However in many cases, most of the efficiency can be achieved at populations of less than 20,000 people.

We also know that for larger metro areas, size does not always mean more efficient. One study shows communities become less efficient with populations greater than 50,000 people. This conclusion is consistent with the County administration cost chart in the Governor's Commission Report.

Other studies also show that cost per citizen varies widely among local units of government of similar size. This is true in Iowa as well. Therefore, it is far more important to provide citizens with the tools for measuring accountability and performance of their local units of government than it is to encourage massive consolidation. Providing citizens with an opportunity to compare the efficiency and performance of their local units of government to others of similar size would have more impact on achieving efficiency and quality of public services across the state than consolidation.

In conclusion, Iowa should not move forward to reorganize Iowa's 99 counties into sub-state units of government based solely on the Governor's Commission recommendations. The Commission's savings estimates are flimsy and the study says nothing about the changes in accountability and local control. At the very least, more detailed studies of the counties most likely to consolidate should be examined in a pilot project to determine whether the savings are real or imagined.

4. Program Cuts Versus Efficiency Gains.

Let's not kid around. Only about $3 million out of $30 million in estimated county consolidation savings and $9 million out of $125 million in estimated school consolidation savings can be called efficiency savings. The rest cannot be attributed to efficiency savings and therefore must be attributed to program cuts or reduction in inputs that can affect performance.

For example, if we increase the statewide pupil/teacher ratio from 15 to 20 as recommended by the Governor's Spending Reform Commission, we end up cutting 6,000 teachers statewide. This proposal only improves school efficiency if (1) schools are presently operated inefficiently or (2) if schools are operating at less than full classroom capacity. In the latter case, consolidation would result in greater efficiency by reducing teaching costs per student and spreading administrative costs over more pupils after the districts consolidate.

However, half of Iowa's school districts are not candidates for consolidation because of their size and location. Secondly, consolidation would not likely be immediate for those that are candidates for consolidation because few school districts rush into consolidation and merger decisions.

This being the case, if the Commission's recommendation were made law, most school districts would immediately make cuts in programs to comply with the proposed policy. There would likely be a return to core curriculum. The courses dropped would likely be those that have low pupil teacher ratios or high cost per pupil, such as special education courses, gifted and talented programs, and vocational instruction.

While citizens may or may not conclude that such cuts are a good thing, the point is that the Commission's final suggestion on schools was labeled as an efficiency measure, but really represented a cut in programs. The moral of the story is that solving the deficit requires real cuts in real programs. Efficiencies from consolidation or government restructuring will not be large enough to do the job.

If this were not the case, political analysts might wonder why we didn't avoid the present budget deficit in the first place because we reorganized state government back in 1987. The point is that state government reorganization didn't slow down state spending nor did it prevent the current budget crisis. In fact, state spending grew more rapidly after consolidation than it did before the consolidation. The events appear to be independent.

Sure, the state of Iowa absorbed the court system from local government, but they also passed 41 pages of new programs since 1987. Suggesting that inefficient local government created the budget deficit or that consolidating local government entities will solve it are conclusions that make headlines but contain little economic validity.

In recent years, Polk County and the City of Des Moines have examined the possibility of city-county consolidation through the auspices of a Charter Commission. Many citizens and leaders found it to be a difficult gut-wrenching experience that requires significant time and resources of local leadership simply to get to the point of making a decision. The same would be true in all other communities across the state. In view of the failure of the

Charter Commission, both rural and urban Iowans should be skeptical about proposals for massive local government consolidation, as suggested by members of Iowa's corporate elite.

While some consolidations do make sense, others do not. The consolidation process can be disruptive in the short run and employee moral and performance can be reduced much more easily than it can be improved. Case studies on business and government consolidations suggest that most consolidations would not have occurred if efficiency was the only criteria. Why? Other factors like control, market power, customer access, and quality of service are often considered to be more important factors.

If that doesn't convince you, here is an example with numbers. Suppose we consolidated all of the smallest school districts in Iowa, those with less than 250 pupils per district. In 1991, this included 51 districts with 27,000 pupils or 12 percent of the school districts. These districts accounted for 1.9 percent of the K-12 pupils in the state.

Next, we assume that we achieve 15 percent cost savings as a result of these consolidations. This is a big assumption because sometimes the added transportation costs will more than offset the reduction in teaching costs. But for the moment, let's assume 15 percent savings. That means 15 percent savings times 1.9 percent of Iowa's pupils. The total statewide estimate would amount to $9 million dollars in savings. Our total education spending in Iowa is $3 billion. So, the savings amounts to three-tenths of one percent of our statewide education bill.

Now this does not mean we should or should not look at ways to improve efficiency. It just simply means that statewide consolidation will not generate a great deal of statewide savings, even if local savings are significant. It is incorrect to conclude that consolidation saves big bucks which can solve our state budget crisis.

5. The Consolidation Process Has Been Ongoing.

The seemingly forgotten facts are that most Iowa school districts have been holding sharing and consolidation discussions for the past seven years. During this period, 153 school district boards—about one third of the total—voted to functionally consolidate operations with another district in the form of whole-grade sharing. As a result, 71 districts have now moved ahead to consider more formal merger by public vote. We are nearing the end of the latest of several rounds of school consolidations that have occurred every two or three decades for the past century.

In other local governments, including cities and counties, the use of 28E agreements have resulted in a wide range of consolidation activities, including consolidation of functions between cities and counties, geographical consolidation of certain functions among counties, and private sector contracting. Unlike schools, county and city governments have many service functions and the economies of size is different for each function. Some services are efficiently organized in sub-county units. Most are efficiently organized in county units, other are more efficiently organized on a multi-county basis.

The economies of size can change as technology, regulations and public policy change. For example, landfills serving six county population areas have become more cost efficient since the passage of the 1989 Iowa Waste Management Act. Landfills serving smaller county or sub-county population areas have become more costly per citizen.

States have taken two approaches in achieving efficient government service for each function. One approach is to set up multiple taxing districts and elect a set of local officials for each service function. Each service function is organized to serve the most efficient size of area and people. As a result, each citizen belongs to several overlapping districts: a sewer district, water district, trash district, etc.

A second approach is more common in Iowa. Iowa has retained the traditional multi-purpose units of county government. We elect one set of local officials who are in turn responsible for overseeing a wide range of local services for a single taxing unit. Under this approach, efficiency can be achieved by developing agreements for joint service delivery and private contracting.

From 1965 to 1991, the Secretary of State has registered 1,674 28E agreements representing private contracting and joint service provision activities among various units of local government in Iowa. This means the average county has 17 contracts and joint service agreements.

While some of the original agreements may no longer be functional, the number of agreements has been increasing rapidly in recent years. Two-thirds of the agreements have been registered during the past decade. So, it is wrong to conclude consolidation has not been occurring in local government. Many obvious efficiencies from operational consolidation in service delivery have already been achieved in many Iowa communities.

If citizens want orderly consolidation to occur, voluntary fiscal incentives and technical assistance should be provided. Restructuring would occur over a period of five to ten years and the time table will be decided by the communities that are involved. Such an approach would provide a more orderly transition to structural change and a more stable system of government as citizens participate in deciding their own course.

6. Another Example of Shifting the Blame.

Well, why has Iowa's political leadership placed local government consolidation on the agenda? As long as the facts surrounding consolidation are not well understood, Iowa citizens will likely accept the status quo notion that grand savings can be achieved by statewide consolidation. Since half of the state budget goes to schools and local government aid, status quo politicians suggest massive local mergers would help solve Iowa's budget deficit. And almost everyone believes them.

In reality, it is another example of misinforming Iowa citizens about what is really feasible. Yes, it is true that local schools and local government will need to adjust to their changing economic and population bases over the next few decades. It is true some savings can be achieved from consolidation. But, it is not true that grand savings are to be had that will solve the budget crisis. We should let the facts drive consolidation, not our emotions and not the agenda of Iowa's corporate elite.

Linking the budget crisis to local government consolidation is a form of smoke and mirrors that focuses public attention on something other than the real causes and solutions of the present budget crisis. Similar to the Taxpayer's Rights Amendment, it becomes another way for status quo politicians to shift the blame to others from the issues at hand. It allows them to say, "we are fiscally responsible" without taking actions that will materially solve the present budget crisis.

If Iowans decide local government consolidation is needed, fine. Let's organize a decade long process. But, let's not convince Iowa citizens that local government is the root of our budget crisis or that massive local government consolidations will solve our budget crisis, because they won't.

7. Privatization and Internal Restructuring.

Before geographic consolidation of counties is considered, it often makes more economic sense to consider internal restructuring, functional consolidation with other local government units and/or privatization. Perhaps there is another local business or another local government division that possesses slack capacity. Maybe they even provide a similar service or function. If so, it may make more economic sense to consider internal reorganization, functional consolidation and privatization than to consolidate geographically with another similar neighboring unit of local government. However here too, these concepts should be approached with both eyes open.

In the case of internal restructuring, savings and improved accountability is not necessarily generated by eliminating a county recorder and five employees if the duties and five more employees are added to the auditor's office and treasurer's office. Replacing the county supervisors, sheriff, treasurer, auditor and recorder with a county council, county manager, and professional staff may or may not increase cost efficiency.

Changing the local government structure under home rule does provide an opportunity to improve the local standard of performance. But the opportunity to improve performance depends in part on how inefficient and how poorly managed the present local government system is performing.

In a similar vein, certain kinds of privatization may not always make economic sense. The government must still maintain ability to audit performance, assure integrity in the services provided, and maintain accountability in the use of the public funds. This may be harder to accomplish when private firms are involved and funds are co-mingled.

In some cases, privatization would inconvenience and increase the time and cost of government functions. In other cases, privatization may not work because the local unit of government may be the only entity with the capacity to make a capital investment to provide a certain local service. The potential for political favoritism and patronage and ethics problems can develop in privatization. In still other cases, privatization may mean one firm is given monopoly control over provision of a service to or for government at the exclusion of other private firms. Such strategies require case by case examination.

For example, the Governor's Commission on Spending Reform recommended privatization of the Iowa fiber optics network. This is an interesting case because in order to start the state-owned network, we pledged to divert state government phone business from private sector phone companies. So on the one hand, Iowa is promoting privatization. However, on the other hand, Iowa is diverting private sector business to create a state-run voice/video communications enterprise.

Iowa already had private sector phone companies laying fiber optics cable in the ground around the state. These capital investments were made on an incremental basis, based on projected local volume and profitability. Now, we have a state-owned enterprise that may compete with the private sector. The state-owned enterprise will have the equivalent of an interstate communications highway to each county seat, whether each county's potential use can economically justify the capacity or not.

The Iowa fiber optics network has the potential to create public sector efficiency and improve the quality of public services, but it will also replace a portion of the potential private sector business that would have existed. The system was promoted as a means for stimulating economic development; however, presently only public TV, state and local government agencies, universities, community colleges and school districts are allowed access to the system.

There is debate over adding the federal agencies, hospitals, local cable TV and local phone companies. Moving this direction would help pay for the system, but it also has the potential to divert additional business away from other private sector companies that have their own fiber optics cable. Eventually, phone companies and cable TV companies will face intense competition for interactive voice and video capability and market share. Recently, U.S. West announced a joint venture with Time-Warner to build a national interactive voice/video fiber optic network. TCI announced similar fiber optic investment intentions. Both would dwarf Iowa's state-owned network.

Within Iowa, our state-owned network has the potential to influence the profitability and structure of the industry. Existence of the network can either enhance communications development or be viewed as competition and slow private sector development.

The state possesses potential unfair advantages if the state-owned fiber optics network is used in direct competition with the private-owned fiber optics network in Iowa. The private companies pay taxes and are highly regulated. The state-owned network does not pay taxes, nor does it appear to be regulated on the same equal basis. If and when Iowa considers re-privatizing its fiber optics network, a level playing field should be attempted. Otherwise, privatization will give unfair advantage to some firms and bring unintended harm to others that have already invested in their own fiber optics capability.

A recent PPEP Focus Group of diverse Iowa leaders and citizens were asked to define what the role of government should be. They developed the following eight criteria. Privatization and restructuring are mentioned; however, the group's principles place these two concepts in broader perspective.

First, the government should be responsive to concerns of the public.

Second, the government should operate within a balanced budget, except in an emergency.

Third, the government is responsible for protecting individual citizen's rights and common interests.

Fourth, government should only provide goods, services and functions that it can provide more efficiently than the private sector or that are required to assure equal opportunity, justice and protection of our individual rights.

Fifth, the government should strive to accomplish all that it can in making itself more efficient before we cut services and functions.

Sixth, the government's challenge is to redesign service delivery and functions first and then to adjust taxes and the tax mix in ways that do not compromise Iowa's competitiveness.

Seventh, government's restructuring processes need to favor self-determination by local communities and regions.

Eighth, government incentives from the state are needed to stimulate reconfiguration of local community services and functions.

8. When Does Consolidation Make Sense?

What are the principles and criteria that business and community leaders use in considering joint ventures, mergers, and consolidations with neighboring institutions? The first step is to identify why the state and/or local government entity would be interested in consolidation to begin with. From my experience with private and public sector consolidation discussions, the following eight questions identify the principles to consider.

First, can you create an opportunity to reduce costs, increase efficiency, and generate operational savings? Logical merger candidates for generating cost savings exist when neighboring institutions are operating duplicate facilities at half capacity. By consolidating the operations of two or more facilities, some operations might be sold or salvaged, while others are operated at full capacity. The capacity is down-sized to the level of demand and may provide up to 20 percent cost savings. The opportunity for consolidation rises when one or more of the facilities has become dated and obsolete.

Second, can you establish a more healthy financial foundation for the future? Two highly leveraged financially weak enterprises do not necessarily make a strong consolidated entity. Therefore, both potential partners must exercise prudent judgment to avoid unintended financial risks and exposure.

Third, can you increase specialization of resources and/or diversification of output? In some cases, consolidation may provide an opportunity to access and retain more specialized and talented employees to improve the quality of services, while providing a wider variety of goods and services to the public.

Fourth, can you create a more dominate economy or marketing position? Can you increase the pool of customers or gain market clout? In the private sector, there are three ways to increase volume: earn it, buy it, or joint venture it. Earning volume is a slow process of out-competing the competition. It involves consumer choice and survival of the fittest. Buying market share requires ability to find bargains and to buyout your competitors.

While some of the private sector joint venturing principles apply to public sector consolidations, others do not. The ground rules and options in public sector joint ventures and consolidation issues are set by state government. Three approaches include mandatory consolidation, voluntary restructuring and mandatory study.

Mandatory restructuring is accepted only at high political costs in the next election, unless the local people can be convinced that the local benefits greatly outweigh the loss. Due to historical convention, local citizens and leaders feel that local institutions are theirs. Suggestions by outsiders from Des Moines or Washington for restructuring are usually unwelcome unless locals can be convinced it will improve their quality of life or the community's future.

Voluntary restructuring provides incentives to encourage merger discussions, but does not require consolidation. Local communities determine who will be their merger partners and the terms of any partnership. The voluntary approach sometimes results in orphan districts and "uneconomic ventures" unless the state retains some veto power over merger proposals.

Mandatory study requires local leaders to set up a study process to evaluate all relevant consolidation options, including continuing the present system. Then, local voters and a state commission are asked to approve or reject the recommendations of the local commission. One option is keeping the present system.

The fifth consolidation principle; do all participants receive fair treatment going into the partnership? If a potential partner is under financial stress, the other partners must exercise prudent judgment to avoid unintended financial exposure. Sometimes independent appraisals, auditors, and consultants can play an appropriate role in evaluating programs, assets, and liabilities of each participant. Escrow accounts may also reduce the risk of financial exposure to contingent liabilities and overvalued assets from other parties.

Sixth, will each participant equitably share the future control and benefits of the joint venture? A variety of voting rules and management structures can be designed to assure the future governance structures respect the interests of the majority as well as the minority interests.

Seventh, will each participant be better off in the partnership than outside of it? If the potential partnership does not meet this goal, the partnership does not make sense.

Finally, will the partnership provide for greater flexibility, care of customers, and innovation in the future? A joint venture partnership simply requires that two institutions pool resources and develop a shared-vision of future control. Whole-grade sharing among schools is an example.

Joint ventures allow two or more entities to achieve operational savings without cut throat competition and risks of financial leverage. Each board retains it's options and flexibility for the future. However, accountability and the decision-making process can become more complex and inefficient with multiple boards or administrative teams making decisions. Joint ventures are often seen as first steps toward full merger.

According to a former professor, the most contentious consolidation issues are likely to be: "How do you value the assets and liabilities? Who is going to be the new CEO? Where is the headquarters going to be?"

9. Who Should Control The Process?

As we step back from the consolidation criteria and look at the whole decision-making process surrounding consolidation decisions, the issue of control becomes important. Who should control the process? Who should decide the minimum standards, the negotiation process, and the structural options considered? Who should decide whether or not to merge? It can be argued that the state has an appropriate role in setting standards, broadly outlining the decision-making process, providing some guidance, and assuring that the structural options considered integrate well with ongoing state government structures. However, decisions on whether or not to consolidate have historically been left to local boards and the voting public.

Historical traditions of community self-determination and local sovereignty on consolidation questions will likely continue. If this is the case, massive mergers of local public institutions will occur only when and if community leaders and citizens decide they are ready for it. To vote "yes," local leaders and citizens must be convinced that consolidation is in their future best interest. State leaders can only create the conditions where structural change is more likely to occur by requiring minimum standards with penalties for noncompliance, and providing state incentives and technical assistance.

Using this concept, the Public Policy Education Project (PPEP) demonstrated that small grants can be leveraged to encourage communities to examine the feasibility of sharing services. The PPEP pilot stimulated a lot of interest and proposals. Since then, the approach has been adopted and modified by the Iowa Department of Economic Development community grant program.

In contrast, the Governor's Commission on Spending Reform recommended that final decisions on local consolidations should no longer be decided by a vote of the public in each taxing unit. They suggested final consolidation decisions be transferred to a local charter commission appointed by state representatives and county officials. This would be a departure from past tradition.

It probably was not coincidence that the 1993 Iowa Senate passed a Des Moines Charter Commission bill that would change public voting rules that would make it easier to set up regional government services. The proposal would have conducted one vote tally instead of two. All taxing units covered by the proposed service would be counted together instead of separately. Individual jurisdictions would no longer have the power to opt out if the whole plan was adopted by a majority of voters in the whole region. This voting process favors the taxing unit with the dominate population size.

The bill was defeated in the House. The Committee Chair indicated more time was needed to study how it would impact all the other counties and cities in the state.

Other political leaders have also suggested cutting state aid to squeeze local government into more consolidation. However, consolidation may or may not result depending upon local circumstances. Local leaders are more likely to give first emphasis to internal efficiency measures. An attempt to examine privatizing, functional consolidations, and/or geographical consolidations may follow. However, the other option is for local leaders to hunker down, make cuts in local programs, retain local service, and retain local community power structure control.

ISU research of local government institutions after the farm crisis suggested that state government strategies of squeezing local government to encourage restructuring may not work. Severe local service quality problems were likely to result from the financial stress. Community leaders under financial stress were less likely to entertain consolidation in the short run compared to other communities with greater human and financial resources.

In recent years, several kinds of multi-district organizations have been formed in many areas of the state. Area Education Agencies, Regional Councils of Government, and more recently, 70 Multi-community Development Organizations have organized as a result of rural leadership training programs.

In some cases, these organizations facilitate consolidation by replacing functions of smaller existing institutions. They increase efficiency by pooling resources to conduct certain functions on a multiple district or regional basis. In other cases, multi-district organizations provide the size economies to develop new or expanded program functions.

However, some become political coalitions seeking new funds to reverse local trends and prevent further consolidation. Therefore, encouraging consolidation by developing multi-district groups does not necessarily result in less state spending.

10. A Layer Cake for Accountability.

As we think about local government consolidation, we must also examine ways to restore accountability in state and local government. Accountability means that government honestly takes citizen input and makes decisions that are perceived to be in the common interest. Accountability means that each government unit possesses a measure of responsibility, independence, authority, flexibility, discretion, funding and self-determination.

According to Steffen Schmidt, ISU political scientist, we used to think our system of federal, state, and local government was a model of accountability. Like a layer cake, each level was responsible for certain functions. However, over time each level of government has taken on part of the functions formerly held by the other levels. As a result, all levels of government have become involved in all functions of government. Each higher level of government places increasing mandates on the lower levels. Local control, discretion and flexibility are reduced as mandates and red tape blur lines of accountability. We now have something that looks more like a marble cake.

There is a need to restore the functions of government and to re-establish accountability using the basic principles of democracy. The principle of self-determination is important. Many citizens believe communities should be able to retain a measure of self-determination and control over their own futures, institutions, and collective investments. This is why most local public institutions cannot be merged without a vote of the people within the local jurisdiction.

Another Jeffersonian principle is "government that is closest to the people is best." Somehow we have lost sight of the diversity possessed by our communities. Each community has different circumstances, problems, resources, opportunities and constraints. The solutions invented by one community for solving its problems will not necessarily work in another. Even more people conclude the solutions invented in Des Moines will not work for all communities. One size does not fit all.

If a function is determined to be a local responsibility, then local control and flexibility should be provided as well. While state and federal government have roles in assuring minimum standards and accountability to the public, local control and flexibility are needed to assure that the local citizenry is served to their fullest benefit given the resource availabilities and local circumstances. Local control and flexibility provides the opportunity to be creative and to pilot new strategies for serving the public more efficiently and effectively.

While it is generally recognized that higher levels of government are more efficient and effective in collecting revenues, lower levels of government are generally more efficient and effective in delivery of goods and services.

In recent years, local government officials have become more concerned about unfunded mandates imposed by the state and federal government which in turn have reduced local discretionary funds. National studies have indicated that local officials in surrounding states are given more discretion and flexibility than Iowa local officials. We must take a closer look at unfunded mandates that impose costs on local government.

For example, many Iowans have noticed that almost every gas station and every unit of local government with underground storage tanks have been digging up the tanks during the past few years. In many cases, local managers were forced to meet new standards by an imposed deadline in order to qualify for cost sharing money. However, in order to meet the deadline, work had to be done before the standards were complete.

As a result, more was spent by cities and counties in order to guarantee that whatever standards passed would be met. This all occurred during a period when state and local government was in a budget crisis. At a minimum, deadlines and the process could have been slowed down to have less budgetary impact on local government and the private sector. In this case, mandates increased local costs above what would have been necessary.

Local government is created by state government. Therefore, local government exists at the pleasure of state government. It is state government's responsibility to be clear about functions and responsibilities retained for itself and those delegated to local government. The home rule authority and state waivers should be expanded so local leaders have flexibility to act when state mandates, regulations, and standards depart from what is known to work locally. The state should be more concerned with outcomes and performance accountability.

Finally, since state formulas are no longer on automatic pilot, there will be a strong periodic need for intergovernmental review of state mandates, revenue sharing, and functions of government. Iowa citizens and state and local officials will need to come to agreement from time to time as to what is appropriate. Intergovernmental reviews followed by town meetings, conferences, and broad public debate should play a key role in deciding what we want from our government, how we want to pay for it, which level of government should be responsible for each function and how it should be organized in the future.

Chapter 5. Solving the Health Care Problem.

1. The Health Care Concerns: It Costs Too Much.

The statistics are becoming more familiar to citizens across the nation. Health care costs represent 14 percent of our Gross Domestic Product (GDP) and it continues to grow. All of our international competitors pay six to nine percent of their GDP for health care. Health costs have grown two to three times the rate of general inflation. So, we have the most expensive health care system in the world and it is getting more expensive. Yet, 34 million Americans or 14 percent of the population have no health insurance. In Iowa, the estimate is 220 thousand uninsured which amounts to seven percent of the population.

Who is hit by rising costs? We all are. In addition to pricing some low and middle income people out of the health insurance market, rising health care costs are increasingly cited as a reason for the lack of U.S. competitiveness in global markets. U.S. automakers claim that health insurance adds $600 to $800 dollars to the cost of each car. New accounting rules required all American businesses to place estimated future health care costs of retirees on 1992 end-of-year balance sheets as a liability. As a result, many corporations cut contributions for health care benefits promised to retirees.

Small businesses face health care premiums with rate structures that are 20 to 30 percent higher than larger employers. Small businesses have faced more rapid increases in premiums compared to large employers. Estimates by the Hay-Huggins Company show administrative expenses account for up to 40 percent of the health insurance costs for firms with four employees or less, while administrative expenses account for 5.5 percent of health benefit costs for employers with over 10,000 employees.

Self-employed business people, farmers, and individual purchasers are hit with a double whammy on health care. First, they normally face higher premium charges than do employer group plans. Second, they are able to deduct only 25 percent of health care premiums on their income tax returns while employees covered by group plans have 100 percent deductibility if the employer pays for employee premiums with before tax dollars.

In 1980, 11 percent of the federal budget went to health care, including the Medicaid and Medicare programs. The Congressional Budget Office projects that health spending will be nearly 20 percent of the federal budget by 1996.

At the state level, the Iowa Department of Management indicates that the state share of Medicaid costs have been increasing at a rate of 10 to 20 percent per year. Since state revenues are only growing about four percent per year, the Department of Management projects that the state share of Medicaid entitlements will absorb all of the annual growth in state revenues by 1996. So, we all are paying the bill.

2. Not Everyone Has Access.

Nationwide and in Iowa one-quarter of the uninsured people are children under age 18. Less than one percent are over age 65. The highest incidence of uninsured are young adults. One-fourth of those age 18 to 24 do not have health insurance.

Lack of access appears to be discriminatory by income rather than race. Nationwide, the uninsured are 77.5 percent white, 17.5 percent black and 5 percent other races. But, 60 percent of the nation's uninsured are below 200 percent of the poverty line. In Iowa, 70 percent of the uninsured are below this mark.

Nationwide and in Iowa, 80 percent of the uninsured have at least one family member who is employed. Over half of the uninsured workers in the nation and in Iowa are employed by small businesses defined as those with fewer than 25 employees. Many companies, including small businesses, are cutting benefits and shifting to part-time workers. Since benefits aren't required for part-time employees, managers see the move as a way to control costs, including rising health care costs. However without employer based benefits, employees face higher individual health insurance rates. Therefore benefits drive a larger employment issue as increasing numbers of citizens attempt to access affordable health insurance and earn a living.

Finally, the uninsured appear to be evenly distributed as a percentage of population throughout Iowa's rural and urban areas. Therefore, health care access is not just an urban problem nor is it just a rural community problem.

3. Rural Concerns About Availability.

Nationally, there is no shortage of health professionals. However in recent years, many rural areas in Iowa and across the nation have expressed concern over the availability of general practitioners in their communities. Iowa health planning experts have indicated that over 160 rural Iowa communities are looking for additional general practitioners to serve their needs.

One reason for the apparent shortage in certain medical professions is that greater monetary and nonmonetary rewards tend to attract many medical students to other areas of medical specialization. When a shortage develops, several years are required to eliminate it because incentives are slow to change, entry into health professions is tightly controlled and it takes nearly a decade of formal training before one can enter practice.

Another reason that availability becomes a concern in rural areas is due to government Medicare and Medicaid reimbursement rates. The government reimbursement rates cover about 60 percent of the provider's actual costs. But for rural physicians and hospitals the Medicare and Medicaid reimbursement rates are an additional 25 percent lower than those for the same procedures of urban providers. Rural areas in Iowa and other states possess a greater share of the senior citizen population covered by Medicare. As a result, compared to the urban doctor, the returns to the rural family doctor after costs are significantly less.

If family physicians are to be attracted to rural communities, Iowa must continue to seek new ways to (1) improve the working conditions for rural medical professionals; (2) improve the monetary and nonmonetary incentives for medical students to choose family practice over other areas of specialization; (3) provide greater incentives to identify general practitioners who will serve in underserved rural areas; and (4) allow medical assistants appropriate flexibility and responsibility for providing care within their scope of practice.

4. Quality Concerns.

Many analysts suggest that since the U.S. has the most expensive health care system in the world we surely ought to have the best quality of health care. While many analysts agree, others suggest there is room for improvement. *Consumer Reports,* among others, suggest that while some U.S. citizens do very well, others are victims of a system that possesses superfluous equipment, conducts unnecessary surgery, over-medicates its patients and prescribes many questionable procedures. Another study by the RAND Corporation found up to 32 percent of four medical procedures were performed for inappropriate reasons.

A recent Rhode Island study suggests that concerns over care quality also result from poor information flow, outmoded quality control systems, too much specialization, and lack of continuity.

In a recent example, an elderly person was under the care of more than 28 different medical professionals over the span of three days. This journey started with the ambulance attendants after calling "911," included the hospital stay, and ended with long-term care professionals. One could imagine that seeing so many professionals in a large urban medical center would be frightening and would leave an impression that no one was addressing the needs of the patient as a whole.

In response to such concerns, managed care concepts have been on the rise. But now, we see growing concerns that certain styles of managed care may reduce the quality of care, may not necessarily reduce costs, and may contribute to cost shifting to other payers. Managed care means that someone other than the patient decides who will provide the treatment, what treatment will be provided, and/or what will be paid for the treatment.

Under one managed care system, a physician is given "gate keeper responsibility" for medicaid patients. Each patient must consult with his or her physician before any treatment can be administered. This case worker approach has been shown to reduce costs by preventing patients from going directly to more expensive emergency room treatment for minor ailments. While the patient's freedom to choose his or her own doctor and treatment is reduced, gate keeper approaches do provide some accountability for public funds that are being used to pay for treatment.

Another managed care scheme, called "shared risk pools," may go too far, however. Here, patients prepay a set monthly fee directly to providers for health care. In this case, doctors are given a financial incentive to under-prescribe care to patients because the cost of the care comes out of the doctor's pocket.

5. Why Have Costs Gone Up?

In 1990, we spent over $2,354 per person per year on health care in the United States. Canada was second highest in the world with $1,683 per person per year or $600 less. Germany spent $1,232 per person. Japan spent $1,035 per person. The United Kingdom spent $836 per person.

There are several different reasons why costs have gone up. The following list is not in order of priority nor does it include all of the causes. It simply provides evidence that many factors are responsible for rapidly rising medical costs.

As you might expect, the highest cost per office visit among industrialized nations is in the U.S. The highest cost per day for staying in the hospital is in the U.S. The highest cost for each of five common medical procedures is in the United States.

However, the U.S. is only the second highest in the average annual earnings for doctors behind Switzerland. The average physician income in Switzerland is $150,322, compared to $132,300 in the U.S. The third highest is $91,244 in Germany.

Health care providers suggest that costs are higher than otherwise would be the case because too much time is spent filling out forms. A recent time and motion study in Rhode Island found that administrative tasks accounted for 39 to 55 percent of the total cost of providing care in nursing homes, hospitals and home health agencies. In one surgeon's practice, half the total collective time of professionals was spent on actual care. The other half was spent on filing, billing, administration, charting, and seeking information.

Today, some clinics have more staff for processing claims and billing than they have for treating patients. A hospital or clinic must deal with several dozen different insurance companies and public agencies to obtain payment for services. Different insurers require different forms and use different criteria for payment. Appeal processes are different for each. Physicians increasingly use computers and employ more people to seek payment. Since 1980, administrative costs in physicians' offices have risen twice as fast as physicians' net incomes.

Also high on the list of reasons for rising costs provided by health care providers is malpractice insurance. Malpractice premiums have been going up at a rapid rate. The U.S. has the highest number of malpractice claims in the world in proportion to population. Malpractice insurance premiums for U.S. doctors are seven times greater than in other industrialized nations.

Cost shifting is another major reason for rising costs that is unique to the U.S. What does cost shifting mean? Since the federal government limits its Medicare and Medicaid payments to about 60 percent of the full costs, the unpaid costs must be covered from somewhere, so they are shifted to other insurers and private payers. As the reimbursement from government gets more out of line, the costs charged to others goes up more rapidly.

Some analysts suggest that private health insurance industry is partially responsible for rising health care costs, claiming it spends too much on marketing and administration. Also, in response to the government limiting Medicare and Medicaid payments, many private insurers have started to limit their payments as well. In turn, this contributes to additional cost shifting, paper work, and administrative procedures for health care providers. As a result, proponents suggest that cost savings from a Canadian style single-payer system and reducing the number of insurers would be sufficient to cover costs of the uninsured.

Insurers point to state mandated coverages. California mandates that acupuncture be covered by insurance plans. In Minnesota, wigs are to be covered. One insurer claims that Minnesota state mandates increased the costs to the consumer by 10 percent.

Drug companies have been accused of ratcheting up prices for profit levels that greatly exceed other U.S. companies. Recent illustrations claim that identical drugs may be sold at a much higher price in the U.S. than what they can be purchased for in many Central and South American or European nations.

There appears to be growing consensus that our health care system places too much focus on expensive high-tech treatments and not enough emphasis on preventative care. In comparison to low-cost preventive health programs, high-tech treatments are often more profitable for providers. Also fueling this view are new studies showing that unhealthy lifestyles and environmental factors may contribute to nearly half of all illnesses.

Providers buy high-tech equipment to compete, instead of sharing services with a neighboring hospital. Once the equipment is purchased, there are economic incentives for using it at full capacity to recover the full costs. In turn, significant medical costs are expended during the last six months of life. Emphasis on prolonging life has been a major priority in medical research and leads to expensive high-tech procedures.

Finally, some analysts suggest our health care market system has failed because consumers are encouraged to buy more health care and insurance than needed. The present system does not give consumers adequate information or incentives to control costs. People always consume more than they otherwise would when they feel they are spending the insurance company's money instead of their own. One study claims that health care spending in the U.S. could be reduced by as much as one-fourth if patients paid most of their own medical bills out of tax free medical savings accounts and if they were given incentives to control costs.

6. A Short List of Reform Principles.

Where do we go from here? There are four economic principles that would represent a positive initial step toward reform. Each would contribute to reducing excessive costs and providing more equal and uniform access to health care.

First, we could consider implementing a uniform claim form and filing process for all insurance companies. A similar uniform claim process is used by the property insurance industry. One should be developed for health claims. As a result, health care providers would have one set of claim forms and payment procedures instead of 100 different ones.

Second, we could change the tax code to provide uniform tax deductibility of insurance premiums for all individuals. We currently allow full tax deductibility for businesses that don't get sick, but not for individual purchasers who do. Uniform deductibility would create a level playing field for self-employed farmers, businesses, and individual purchasers who are penalized by the present tax code.

Third, we could consider developing a standard minimum benefit package and a uniform method of graduated means testing for Medicare and private insurance coverages. This process would involve public prioritization of health care benefits and develop societal consensus regarding public responsibility versus private responsibility. Surveys show a large majority of Iowans agree that all citizens should have access to a minimum level of health care. Developing a standard package would reduce paperwork and would assure more uniform and equal coverage for all citizens.

The future tradeoff will be in deciding which health care benefits are truly necessary and which ones are discretionary. All discretionary benefits are likely to become an individual responsibility, purchased according to the patient's ability to pay and/or purchased with separate private insurance. But someone must still decide the portion of necessary benefits which should become individual responsibility versus those to be covered by insurance. Then once the decisions are made, we must be careful not to load the system back up with lots of benefits that really should be discretionary.

Fourth, we should have nondiscriminatory uniform pricing of health care. When people buy items in a grocery store, the store does not charge one price for green-eyed people and another price for blue-eyed people. That would add paper, bureaucracy, and administrative cost. But today, some health care providers charge private payers more than double the amount paid by the government or insurers with negotiated rates.

We presently do not have a system that requires a provider to charge the same price to all customers. As a result, neither market discipline nor government can hold providers fully accountable against arbitrary price discrimination. In fact, government has contributed to the problem. Our present system results from cost shifting largely by government to those with the least market clout and ability to negotiate rates. We need a system where providers charge the same price to all customers, regardless of who pays the bill. To eliminate cost shifting, the government must be required to sit at the table and abide by this policy, too.

7. Public Judgment Is Key to Structural Reform.

A recent international survey indicates that 60 percent of our population believes our health care system needs fundamental change. This was higher than any other of the industrial nations surveyed, which implies that perhaps our health care concerns may require system-wide change. Iowa citizens, similar to other citizens in the nation, want our health care system fixed.

Washington has introduced a multitude of health care reform bills in recent years. Congress is geared up for a major nationwide decision on health care. President Clinton has made health care reform one of his top priorities.

Similarly, Iowa has passed numerous health care and insurance bills during the past few years. An early 1993 Iowa Poll of the *Des Moines Register* indicated Iowans ranked health care and jobs as top priorities.

But hold the phone! In a strong democracy, it is a mistake to assume automatically that the solution to health care and insurance will emanate from Washington or Des Moines. It is a mistake to conclude automatically that citizens and communities should not have a say on the kind of health care system they want. With so many different proposals with opposing philosophies, one national or state solution is not likely to be supported by a broad majority of all communities and citizens.

An early perception was that the President would propose a single national health insurance plan without much debate. This would have been a mistake. Yes, the federal government should play a leadership role in setting goals to assure all citizens access to basic, high quality, affordable health care. Uncle Sam should provide principles and incentives for reform, flexibility for states to conduct pilot programs, uniform health benefits taxation, and uniform reimbursement for providers. But that's it.

State government has a leadership role, too. The state has a role in providing voluntary incentives for community-based reform, setting statewide quality standards, and assuring they are met. But, if we truly want health care and insurance reform to be a success, we must educate our community leaders, local providers and citizenry, outline the various options, provide an appropriate period of debate, and involve them in the policy making process community by community.

Until recent months, it almost appeared that citizens were waiting for the new President to solve the problem for us. This is a horrendous expectation to place on any President. The traditional democratic way is for we the people to educate ourselves and develop our own sense of what works in our communities and in our lives. If we cannot figure out the solutions, how is the President going to figure it out? Good Presidents listen to the people.

We have historically relied on citizen education and popular ballot to make school and local government structure decisions. If citizens, providers, and community leaders are given the opportunity to select the health care and insurance structure they prefer, they are more likely to take charge and make it succeed. What works in northwest Iowa may not fly in southeast Iowa. What works in urban Iowa may not fly in rural Iowa. This is evidenced from years of experience with diverse community leaders.

8. Why Consider Community-Based Solutions?

Since World War II, the government has encouraged the development of employer-based group insurance plans. Since then, premiums and medical costs paid for by employer group plans have been fully deductible by the employer as a cost of doing business. However, self-employed farmers and small businesses and individual purchasers only have partial deductibility. This differential tax treatment has fostered a system that favors the development of employer-based groups in purchasing health insurance.

Why has the access problem developed? Over the decades, competitive incentives encouraged the employer-based plans to move from community rating to group experience rating. Community rating means the insurance premiums are based on the average health experience of the community. Experience rating means the insurance premiums are based on the average health experience of the employer group. Under experience rating the employer and insurance company have an incentive to eliminate individuals with high health risks from employer group coverage, particularly if they have pre-existing health problems or high risk conditions. This shifts the costs to high risk employees who must then purchase individual private insurance at higher premium rates on their own and/or to the public insurance programs for those who cannot afford their own insurance.

With the development of international competition, many Fortune 500 companies and other businesses find that their health benefits are more expensive than that of their international competition. At the same time, the average worker will change employers several times during their career. Under the present employer-based system, an employee risks losing affordable health benefits every time he or she changes jobs. As a result, many businesses and employees are beginning to question the merits of an employer-based private health insurance system.

There are several structural options. We must decide whether we favor regulatory approaches on employers and insurers like mandated benefits and mandated coverage of excluded groups. Alternatively, we could favor putting more responsibility on individuals by requiring all citizens to possess minimum health insurance coverage. Or finally, we could simply assure universal access by moving away from an employer-based group insurance system to a geographical-based group insurance system.

Before we adopt a one-solution-fits-all approach, why not consider a variety of approaches to see which ones work best? Designers of state and federal health care and insurance solutions have publicly admitted their plans may not work well in rural states. The Managed Competition concept considered by the Clinton Administration was designed for communities with over 50,000 in population. Some of its authors suggest the concept might not work well in rural areas. I am not so sure.

The concept applied in rural areas has been renamed Managed Cooperation. Under managed competition, Health Insurance Purchasing Cooperatives (HIPC) would bargain on behalf of consumers with Organized Delivery Systems (ODS) of health care providers. HIPCs and ODSs can take on a variety of sizes and structures depending on community size and needs. Most rural communities are familiar with cooperatives. Most of the concepts proposed can be adapted to community-based institutions. However, they have not been pilot tested. It seems appropriate for rural states like Iowa to conduct pilot demonstrations.

The effectiveness of federal and state solutions versus community-based solutions is an open question, not a foregone conclusion. Compared to national health insurance or state insurance pools, community-based solutions are likely to be more responsive to local needs and would provide local flexibility.

Iowa citizens have been lulled into believing health care is so complex that we should let the experts solve the problem. If we believe in democracy, nothing could be further from the truth. Instead, we should roll up our sleeves, use our heads, and study the issues. If we don't, you can rest assured that no one else will be looking after the interests of the average citizen.

In the next four sections, community-based systems are described. Each concept is patterned after ideas promoted by policymakers and coalitions of Iowa interests. Each could be designed to assure coverage for all citizens. Each could be called a local health care purchasing cooperative or organized delivery system, depending upon how each was chartered. Using the following options, community leaders, local providers, and citizens could choose to charter one of several new institutions. Most analysts already presume that each concept would work in urban areas, so the examples are discussed in terms of how they might work in a typical rural Iowa county.

While I do not necessarily endorse all of the plans, I do endorse the right of citizens to participate in a public judgment process. If we are going to consider health care to be a right of all citizens, citizens should be able to participate in the process. Most of the concepts which have been debated at the state or national level can be converted into community-based solutions that would provide local community control, local flexibility, citizen responsibility, and public judgment.

9. Option 1: A Community-Based Safety Net.

During the 1992 General Assembly, the Iowa Senate passed a statewide safety-net insurance pool that would place uninsured Iowans into a single statewide insurance pool with all public employees. A community-based safety net insurance pool would be the same concept only applied on a county or multi-county basis.

How would it work? The average rural county has about 10,000 people. Assuming even distribution of uninsured people across Iowa, there would be about 700 uninsured people in this rural county example that would be placed into the pool. We could add families of the self-employed small business people, farmers, and individual purchasers of health insurance who would be interested in achieving lower premium costs.

The pool could also add local people with high risk costs assuming that state subsidies were transferred to the pool. City, county, and school employees could also be added to the pool under the principle that each group would have to be better off in the new larger pool than outside it. All other citizens in the county would continue to pay for and receive health insurance through their employer groups if they desired to do so.

The bottom line is that a community-based health insurance pool with more than 2000 people could be formed in the average rural county in Iowa. Such an insurance corporation or cooperative would have size economies of many large employer groups that presently have lower premium rates.

Second, if the premiums are collected as an adjustment to state income or property taxes, they become fully deductible for farmers and self-employed persons on their federal income taxes.

Third, the paperwork and administrative costs for rural hospitals and health care providers are reduced as the number of different insurance forms and insurance procedures are reduced.

Who would pay for the uninsured? Presumably, citizens receiving access to minimum health care benefits would pay according to their ability and the remainder would come from the government. Similar to the statewide safety net plan, the remainder would come from general statewide or national tax sources. Public employees or other members of the local pools should not be required to pay any more than citizens outside of the pool to cover the uninsured population.

In counties where there is only one hospital, the hospital represents a local monopoly in performing most health care functions. The county-wide safety net would organize rural health consumers in a fashion that would increase their relative marketing power. Balancing local market power would become an important factor in negotiating and defining local health care needs, in controlling costs, and in maintaining profitability of rural health providers. Local health care costs would more likely be controlled as local employers and the local Community Health Insurance Purchasing Coop or Corporation bargained on more equal footing with the local health care providers.

10. Option 2: A Community-Based Single-Payer System.

In contrast to the Senate proposal, the Iowa House passed a Canadian-style single-payer system during the 1992 General Assembly. In the rural community example, all 10,000 county residents would be required to pay into a county-wide or multi-county insurance corporation. Premiums become fully deductible for self-employed farmers, small business people, and individual purchasers if they are collected as adjustments to income or property taxes. The adjustments to state or local taxes would replace all other present health insurance premiums.

Employers might also be required to pay a payroll assessment distributed according to the residence of its employees. However, the employer would not have health care benefits to manage. This function would be transferred to the Community Health Insurance Purchasing Coop or Corporation. Local businesses could place more focus on management, labor, and resources on producing quality products and profits.

A community-based single-payer insurance corporation would have greater economies of size than the previous safety-net pool and may possibly provide premium rates lower than those currently provided by large employers because there would be less spent on marketing costs. In addition, the paperwork and administrative overhead costs for rural hospitals and health care providers would be significantly cut as the number of different insurance forms and insurance procedures are reduced to one.

Finally, the community-based single payer concept would organize rural health consumers. The Community Health Insurance Corporation or Cooperative would possess market power equal or greater than that of the rural health care provider. This kind of control would become an important factor in defining local health care needs, in controlling costs, and in maintaining profitability of rural health providers.

11. Option 3: A Community Organized Delivery System.

The Iowa Leadership Consortium (ILC) was a group of prominent Iowa health care providers, insurers, and large employers organized and underwritten by Blue Cross and Blue Shield of Iowa. This consortium studied Iowa's health care issues for two years and presented its plan in 1992 for public discussion. The ILC recommended that an Iowa Health Commission of seven people be established with statewide authority to (1) set price control targets and regulate payments to all providers; (2) to implement a statewide play or pay insurance plan; and (3) to encourage and contract with local Organized Delivery Systems.

The "play or pay" concept requires all employers to provide a minimum set of health benefits for all employees or pay a tax equal to five percent of the payroll toward purchasing employee coverage from a private insurer or a statewide health insurance pool. Universal access would be provided to all citizens because the proposal would require all individuals to have insurance.

An Organized Delivery System (ODS) would be a new private sector institution. One version of the concept could be created by having all employers within a county or multi-county area join area hospitals and providers in forming a new corporation. This new corporation would self-insure or contract with an outside insurance company to manage benefits of those covered under the system. The state would contract with ODSs to care for uninsured people in the local community.

Self-employed farmers, small businesses, and individual insurance buyers could join the ODS at rates likely to be lower than the present system. However, premium costs would not be fully deductible for income tax purposes without changes in federal tax laws.

Because of the economies of size required to be efficient, most rural areas would likely be part of only one Organized Delivery System. Each citizen and/or his or her employer would pay a monthly premium for health benefits. The benefit management function could be transferred from the local employers to the local ODS. The local hospital, clinics, and doctors belonging to the ODS would provide the care. A central benefits office would collect the premiums, manage the costs and benefits, invest the reserves, and pay health care professionals according to predetermined fee schedules. Risks and profits would be shared by all investors. This shared-risk pool concept would likely prevent cost shifting.

Administrative, marketing, and overhead costs would be reduced compared to the present system. There would be only one major insurer in the area, one set of forms, one set of procedures in each Organized Delivery System.

Finally, it is unclear whether the interests of the health professionals, insurers, employers, consumers or stockholders would dominate in the management of the ODS and in defining local health care needs. Under some shared-risk pools, physicians are given an incentive to cut costs and under-prescribe care. In other cases, managed care systems save money and provide care standards that prevent such occurrences.

12. Option 4: Consumer Incentive and Cost Recovery.

This approach borrows concepts from the Heritage Foundation proposal to strengthen and continue the present system. Historically, county government has been responsible for providing indigent care expenses for those without health insurance and without the ability to pay for health care. In more recent years, the state and federal government began to provide health care for the poor through the Medicaid program. Under this option, the present system would continue, but local government would be given increased powers to recover costs from individuals without insurance coverage and to initiate managed care arrangements with local providers for the indigent.

Second, government would provide increased tax incentives for all citizens to make monthly payments into a tax-free medical savings account that could only be used to pay health care bills. This approach would encourage individuals to self-insure and directly pay most of their regular medical expenses. Insurance would only be needed for more catastrophic illnesses.

One national study suggests that nearly half of the first $1000 spent on medical expenses per individual goes to paper pushing, administration and bill paying costs. The study suggests we have a tendency to buy more health insurance than we need. It suggests the major reason health costs are increasing is consumers enter the health care marketplace feeling like they are spending someone else's money instead of their own. It concludes that since we don't hire a third party to pay for regular food, clothing and utility expenses, why should we hire an insurance company to pay for the regular portion of our medical expenses?

By moving to tax free medical savings accounts and higher deductibles for catastrophic insurance, a portion of the insurance company's bill paying costs could be saved directly by the consumer. Citizens would be paying more of their regular health care bills. Their health care spending would become more frugal. We are always more frugal when we spend our own money.

13. Emphasize Innovation and Pilot Testing.

Each community-based concept above is based on a different philosophy. Each option could potentially contribute to controlling costs and expanding coverage. But we have no way of knowing which system will work best in the eyes of communities and citizens unless we conduct pilot demonstrations. Parts of each concept could even be combined into a fifth option.

For example, Managed Competition/Cooperation models considered by the Clinton Administration combine elements from Options 1, 2 and 3. Instead of having one statewide Iowa Health Care Commission as recommended by the Iowa Leadership Consortium, there would be local Health Care Purchasing Coops that would negotiate with local Organized Delivery Systems. This model provides more balance between consumer and provider interests in comparison to the ILC Health Commission model.

The distinguishing characteristic between a cooperative and a corporation is that in a cooperative, customers own the business and sit on the board of directors. Other than board-management structure, coop business functions are similar to corporations. What we call an Organized Delivery System or Health Care Cooperative is still an open question. Various hybrid structures for dispersing power among providers, insurers, employers, and consumers are still possible. Such functions can become coops or corporations.

In the final analysis, we are simply shifting benefits, management, accountability, and payment functions among employers, corporate insurers, providers, and consumer interests. The real question is how to balance the interests to be represented on the boards if we are to provide accountability, access, and quality of care at a more reasonable cost?

In fact the 1993 Iowa General Assembly passed a bill that would allow several different variations of Health Insurance Purchasing Cooperatives (HIPCs) and Organized Delivery Systems (ODSs) to be tried. After the pilot experiments are evaluated, community leaders and average citizens gain experience and would tend to move toward systems that work the best for them. Iowa will gain a sense of direction from our own communities and citizens. Over time, successful demonstrations will become more widely adopted.

14. Who Should Make the Policy Decisions?

Perhaps the most important issue raised by the various approaches discussed above is who should control our health care and insurance benefits system? In addition to deciding whether insurers, providers, employers, and consumer interests should dominate the decision process, we must also decide whether the decisions should be made at the federal, state, or local level.

The Iowa Health Care Leadership Consortium (ILC) recommended a system of organized delivery systems to operate under a single seven-member Iowa Health Commission. The Commission would be established to regulate Iowa's $7 billion dollar health care and insurance industry. The recommended Commission membership includes a doctor, hospital administrator, allied health professional, insurance representative, large group employer, a small group or individual purchaser, and a health economist.

The proposed Iowa Health Commission membership raises concerns about potential conflicts of interest in making future health care policy decisions. We don't allow utility representatives to sit on the utility commission. We don't let teachers and administrators sit on the school board. Should insurers, physicians, and hospital administrators be different?

One concludes the ILC proposal might become dominated by big health, big insurance, and corporate interests not unlike the Consortium membership itself. Twenty-five of thirty-six ILC members were from Polk county. Only six came from the 86 most rural counties with half Iowa's population. There were not many people from places like Manning or Strawberry Point.

Citizens should ask for the rationale of having a single state or federal commission structure to set price controls and provider payment rates. We have a national currency, so there are merits for a Federal Reserve Board. There are merits for state commissions to regulate public utilities and other regional monopolies. But do similar compelling reasons exist for a single state or federal health commission? Or is health care similar to education, which is locally demanded and locally supplied? If this is the case, placing the state commission between local health consumers and local providers may simply add to the system dysfunction when decisions could be made locally.

Each of the 220,000 uninsured Iowans and each of the 35 million uninsured Americans live in a community-based trade area of one or more local health care providers. Regional control is needed only when services become more specialized.

For comparison, Iowans have decided K-12 education—which is only a $3 billion industry—is too important to place under the control of a single state board. Iowa has one state board and over 400 local school boards to assure universal access, manage quality, and control costs. If something goes wrong the citizens know whom to call. Additional regional and state boards are organized for institutions with regional specialization or statewide higher education service provision. The Legislature and Governor have not delegated funding decisions and payment systems for education to any specialized commission.

What are the likely consequences of having control vested in a single seven member Iowa Health Commission compared to having control vested in a system of 99 Community Coops or Corporations? Under the single commission concept, most citizens would have more difficulty in contacting state Commissioners when something went wrong. They would likely end up calling their state legislator or congressional representative. The Commission would likely be less responsive to individual citizen concerns than concerns of policymakers, large health providers, insurers, or interest group lobbyists. If state or national health insurance pools are established, only large insurers would likely be able to demonstrate capacity to bid on managing the insurance pools.

Under the dispersed local control system, citizens know whom to call locally if there is a problem. Local board members are more likely to act. If 99 Health Purchasing Coops are set up, small insurers would have 99 opportunities to bid for part of the state health insurance market. This creates a more level playing field for large and small insurers, communities and citizens.

Since Iowa's rural communities have a disproportionate share of senior citizens who tend to have greater health care needs, the community-based approaches are ready made $5 to $10 million dollar rural development opportunities that rural communities would not want to pass up. Instead of solutions that create new bureaucracies and build new buildings in Washington and state capitals, why not put the employees closer to where the problems are? This would strengthen the ability of local communities to assure universal access, provide quality, and control costs. With today's communication technologies, this system could be as efficient and would provide opportunity for citizen input and local control.

15. What Has Iowa Done?

In recent years, Iowa has created several statewide insurance pools for those who meet specific entitlement criteria. As a result, a few more uninsured people are covered each year. If current trends continue, health care decisions will become more dominated by state policymakers and special interests instead of community leaders and citizens.

After suggesting the Iowa Health Care Leadership Consortium did not contain enough rural representation, the Governor appointed a 56 member Commission to study health care during 1993. But only 13 of the members of the Governor's Commission reside in Iowa's 86 rural counties that account for half of Iowa's population. Iowa's 13 largest counties, which account for the other half of Iowa's population, garnered 77 percent of the representatives on the Governor's Health Care Commission.

Interestingly, 26 members or 46 percent of the Governor's Commission reside in Polk County. Polk County has four times the number of representatives justified on the basis of population. For comparison, the Governor's Commission is 23 percent rural. The Leadership Consortium was 16 percent rural. So it was an improvement, but both health care study groups had less than half the rural representation justified on population.

Staff reports show Commission membership at 28 percent health administrators, 17 percent doctors, 17 percent public officials, 13 percent business, 9 percent insurers, 7 percent lobbyists, 6 percent consumers and 3 percent other. Consumer and small business interests voiced concern over representation.

Having presented this breakdown, it must also be said that a lot of hard work has gone into both efforts. Most of the participants are well respected leaders. Some people residing in Polk county represent rural interests. Both the members and staff spent a lot of time, hard work and money.

However the average citizen can figure out that proposals favored by special interest representatives may not likely pass representative democracy groups—like the legislature—selected according to one-person, one-vote.

For example, national surveys showed a 75 percent majority of citizens favored consumer choice in selecting a provider. Yet, the Governor's Commission twice narrowly voted down this concept as a guiding principle of reforming Iowa's health care system. A similar proposal to emphasize education of health consumers also was defeated twice by the Commission. A more representative body of citizens would likely have passed these principles. It would be unfortunate if Commission proposals are dead on arrival to the Legislature simply because of the way appointments were made.

Perhaps the Senate, House and the Governor could have split the appointments three ways. Perhaps the special interest dominance should have been reduced. Perhaps principles suggested in Chapter 3 should have been followed. Perhaps state agency people should have been made ex-officio and non-voting.

Since this was not done, doubts are raised about whether the proposals developed will represent a consensus of the people or just a consensus of the Governor's Commission. Citizens are left wondering whether appointments were made to control the outcomes or to influence future campaigns. All of these appearances could have been avoided if Jeffersonian principles had been used in appointing the commission members.

Who should control our health care? This is the major policy issue that will likely determine the outcome of the other policy questions discussed in this chapter. If we choose state or national solutions, control will be shaped by state and national lawmakers dominated by well financed special interests. If this path is chosen, a case can be made for increasing rural representation, particularly in state level decisions for Iowa. However, if successful community-based models can be developed, the citizen public choice model would accomplish health care reform, preserve local control, and strengthen our democracy.

Chapter 6. Keeping Iowa Number 1 In Education.

1. What Are The Education Concerns?

Business people complain that new employees who are recent high school graduates cannot read, write, or solve simple math problems related to their jobs. Graduates don't seem to take pride in their work. There doesn't seem to be any performance accountability in the system.

Elementary teachers are concerned that Susie or Sam comes to school hungry without breakfast. So, he or she is not ready to learn. Some children aren't ready to learn because their parents both work and/or are divorced. These parents didn't have time to read to the children and many times the children were left home alone. Some teachers say the first priority for new technology in Iowa classrooms is a phone, so teachers can call parents to get them involved in their children's education performance and progress.

High school teachers are concerned that many students don't respect authority as they once did. Students don't try very hard. They are preoccupied with their part-time jobs, home life, or extracurricular activities; they don't see the value of a quality education. Teachers ask whether Iowa deserves first in the nation education status, given the state has slipped from 19th to over 30th in educational spending per pupil since 1983.

Parents are concerned whether their children are learning anything worthwhile in school and if they will receive a good education in the local school. Will they grow up and be able to think for themselves, be responsible citizens and become community leaders? Will they get pregnant and become parents, use drugs, or become involved in crimes? Are they performing well enough to get jobs or be successful in college? If they aren't, is it the teachers' fault, the school's fault, or children's fault? Parents want their children to be able to be productive, earn an income, and have the same or better standard of living than they have. Parents want children to be happy and to live fulfilling and productive lives.

Students are under different pressures and societal standards than their parents were in school. Some students wonder why they should get an education or work hard in school if they think they cannot find good jobs after graduation. Others are hopeful and do work hard. With so much change in Iowa's economy, students wonder what the future holds and if they will be able to remain in the state.

Community leaders are concerned about creating high-paying jobs that will attract and retain bright young people in local communities. Many leaders believe that we are teaching too many students to become employees instead of how to start businesses, take risks, and become entrepreneurs. Iowa ranks 33rd among states in percent of the population with high school diplomas. Iowa ranks 40th for those with 2-year degrees and 45th for those with 4-year college degrees. This underscores concern about the future income-generating capacity of many Iowa communities.

Taxpayers are paying the bill for education. While they may believe that education is important, many have seen indicators of declining performance over the decades while spending rose. They want accountability. They want assurance their schools are providing a high quality educational opportunity. They want assurance their students are performing as well as the neighboring districts. Increasingly, they want assurance that their schools are doing as well as the Germans and Japanese. And they don't want to pay a dime more for it than they have to!

National leaders and educators are concerned about the two decade long erosion of standardized test scores and the poorer performance of our students relative to Japanese and German students on standardized math and science tests. Many predict the apparent decline in our educational performance will mean erosion of our international competitiveness as a nation.

Iowa leaders and educators agree that our education system is not broken. Far from it. Iowa continues to rank 1st in the nation among the 50 states on standardized test scores. Our rank has been no fluke. Iowa has been at the top or near the top of national standardized tests for decades.

Then why all of this talk about change and transformation? Well, Iowa's test scores, like the rest of the nation, have also eroded during the two most recent decades. Our students have been weak in math and science compared to the Germans and Japanese. However, there are hopeful signs that test scores are beginning to turn around. We know we can do better.

Several national and Iowa business and education interests have suggested that perhaps we have become too complacent. One group suggests we are providing a 1950's style education which was appropriate for the times, but our kids will need a 2010 style education to get the high-paying jobs of the future. Most of the changes in technology experienced during the last 50 years have been things that we could see working, play with, and then understand. Most of the technological changes that will come during the next 50 years will have to be accepted on face value. The technology will be too small or complex for non-experts to rip apart and figure out. Presently, most people hop in their car and turn the key. They are at a loss to do much if the car doesn't run. The average person can no longer lift the hood, change the oil, and repair it as he or she once did.

The point is, all the technology and information based products will be produced somewhere else. Unless we as a nation and we as a state make the investments in education, our children will not have the capability to be the innovators, creators, and producers of tomorrow's goods and services. The bottom line is that Iowa still is first in the nation in education. Our education system is not broken. But, there has been growing concern that we need change to make the best better.

2. Keeping Iowa Number 1: Learning Must Be First.

From a quick reading of hometown newspapers, it appears that many Iowa communities place a higher value on achievement in sports than academics. If this is a signal we don't want our children to receive, it is up to us to bring more balance to the signals we do send. We all want our children to be sociable, well-rounded, and involved in various activities. However, first things first. The first thing we are paying for is learning.

What learning results do we want our schools to accomplish? A 1991 Iowa Business and Education

Roundtable Report titled *World Class Schools: The Iowa Initiative*, represents a thoughtful attempt to capsulize the performance outcomes many Iowans would like to see in our education system. The ideas of business people are important if we want them to hire our high school and college graduates. Their suggestions are:
(1) Each student should be able to read, write, speak, listen and to use math and foreign language skills in ways similar to those they will encounter in life.
(2) Each student should be able to apply core concepts and principles from subjects like mathematics, sciences, humanities, arts, social studies and practical living studies to situations and problems similar to those they will encounter in life.
(3) Each student should become a self-sufficient individual and a responsible member of a family, work group and community.
(4) Each student should be able to think and solve problems both in school situations and in a variety of situations similar to those they will encounter in life.
(5) Each student should be able to connect and integrate experiences and new knowledge from all subject matter fields with what they have already learned.
(6) Each student should have an opportunity to successfully complete a high school education.
(7) Each student should be able to make a successful transition to the work place or postsecondary education institution after high school graduation.

These education goals appear to be fairly reasonable, broad and well-rounded. They are focused on learning outcomes and decision-making. They appear to be void of political or religious bias. The goals do not appear to have a bias for or against diversity or environmentalism. The approach appears to stress building individual character and judgement skills through discussion, examination of various views and case studies in problem-solving, in contrast to philosophical indoctrination of one view. Such group decision and discussion processes would appear to strengthen Jeffersonian democratic principles.

How then should the mix of subjects and skills be changed to attain these education goals? Some suggest that we ought to get back to the basics. Others suggest that we need more math and science. Still others feel that many schools have focused on college preparation at the expense of the other half of the student body who will be looking for jobs right out of high school. Each may be right for a different segment of the student population. The beauty of the Business Roundtable Report is that it challenges us to think ahead about the diversity of goals, talents, and circumstances students will likely encounter in life.

In 1991, the Iowa Public Policy Education Project (PPEP) asked over 200 parents geographically distributed across Iowa to indicate areas they would like to see emphasized in the school curriculum. Out of 30 potential skills and subjects, the parents listed the following ten priorities: (1)English, reading and writing; (2) speech and oral communications; (3) computers and information management; (4) problem solving; (5) study skills; (6) job market training and entrepreneurship; (7) basic science, environment, and conservation; (8) family and parenting skills; (9) vocational math; and (10) advanced technology education.

Parents are fairly consistent with the views of several other recent studies by Iowa education interests. We want our schools to teach our kids what they will need to know tomorrow.

3. A New Commitment to Early Childhood Education.

Presently, 90 percent of the cost of pre-school education programs is funded by parents and ten percent is funded by the public. In Japan and Germany, the reverse is true. There the public pays most of the bill and parents pay less than half. In this country, Head Start programs reach only 33 percent of the children who meet the present income eligibility requirements.

It is a community and public responsibility to give at-risk children from low income families an opportunity to succeed in school and in life. Several studies have shown that $1 spent on early childhood education programs will save at least $5 down the line in terms of remedial programs and costs to society. Money spent to cover children from low income families who are eligible is money well spent as an investment in our future.

4. Respect Good Teachers and Honor Commitments.

The teacher is the most important employee in a school. Most successful citizens and leaders can trace their success to one or more teachers who took the time and cared enough to make a difference in their lives. Teachers are molding the lives of our future leaders and citizens. Our future successes as a state and as a nation depend upon how successful teachers are in what they do. The worth and accomplishments of teachers are much greater than the pay and community recognition they normally get.

In a recent election campaign, gubernatorial candidates made commitments to bring teacher salaries up to the national average. While some gains were made, Iowa's average teacher salary remains below the national average. For 1991-92, Iowa ranks 30th in teacher pay according to the Iowa Department of Education. Iowa's political leadership has not kept its commitment to Iowa teachers. Keeping commitments is an important lesson most parents want their children to learn, and our children learn by example.

If Iowans expect to remain first in the nation in education performance, Iowa leaders and citizens should develop a plan to make good on our state's commitment to improve teacher pay. If we cannot keep our commitment to our teachers, perhaps we should not expect to keep Iowa first in the nation in education.

As part of this commitment, however, Iowa leaders and citizens have the right to insist on rigorous standards of professionalism and excellence. It used to be said that "good teachers are worth their weight in gold." This statement is still true today. We know that many teachers consistently do a better job than others in stimulating learning and generating student performance. Good teachers should be rewarded for their performance.

On the other hand, we cannot afford to have less than competent teachers in the classroom. Teachers should be evaluated as objectively as possible on teaching effectiveness and student learning. Systems that pay teachers the same regardless of performance should be changed. We should be less concerned with the number of degrees or length of service a teacher has and more concerned about the teacher's classroom performance and student learning performance.

5. Create Flexibility and Incentives For Innovation.

If teachers are going to be held accountable for their teaching and learning performance, they must be given control and responsibility over the learning environment, control over the factors that motivate students, and time to prepare. We should encourage creative teaching strategies involving parents, teacher exchange programs, training on new technology in the classroom, and time to plan and test innovative programs.

In recent years, many Iowa education professionals have concluded that we have a "top down system." Too much control is on top and not enough authority and flexibility in the trenches. They say we need to turn the system upside down on its head. The teacher has the most important responsibility in the school system.

Schools with motivated teachers usually have at least one thing in common. They have a determined principal who takes pride in the achievements of the students. They have a principal who strives to organize and create a working environment where teachers perform at their peak. We can neither hamstring our principals and teachers anymore than we can allow incompetent or unaccountable ones to stay on the job. Principals and teachers must have the flexibility to do their job, yet they must be held accountable, too.

School management problems develop when we add new subjects or integrate new skills into existing courses. The Iowa parents surveyed by PPEP wanted 10 new areas of emphasis. They picked only one skill out of the 30 mentioned that should receive less emphasis. What are we going to drop? There are only so many class periods in the day and so many days in the school year under the current system. Local school boards and administrators should give principals, teachers, and parents flexibility and encourage them to experiment with innovative programs that reflect what our children will need to know in the future.

Some teachers may need new educational challenges and retraining. Some schools are trying longer school days and year-round use of buildings. Others are organizing Japanese or German style schools. Some are developing joint programs with local business firms.

At the same time we encourage innovation, we must also have accountability. Some ideas won't work. Performance must be measured so that we can determine which innovations work and which ones do not. The highest cost of an idea that doesn't work may be in terms of lost student achievement. This is particularly true if a bad idea is promoted as a success to other schools.

6. Pilot Demonstrations Before Expensive Technology.

In the future, schools may become more specialized in certain areas of instruction. Why? Certain vocational and advanced technology courses simply require equipment that will be too expensive for one district to justify for the number of students interested. Why not pool resources with neighboring districts to form magnet programs at a central location? This approach has worked in urban areas and other rural states; why not try a few pilot programs in Iowa?

Iowa's biggest gamble related to education is the new fiber optics network. My statements in a *Des Moines Register* editorial on March 10, 1991, still hold: the fiber optics network has the potential to place Iowa at the cutting edge of technology or to become the biggest boondoggle in state history.

I suggested several questions that prudent leaders should answer before construction moved ahead. How many local schools will use the system? How much local financial support is there? How many other private users are there and how much are they willing to pay? These questions still have not been fully answered. So, the jury is still out regarding the outcome of Iowa's fiber optics network.

We do know for sure that 2,500 miles of fiber optics have been laid in the ground around Iowa and we have spent $112 million on a project that was originally supposed to cost $30 million. The total cost including local equipment, access, and initial program charges may run up to nearly $300 million before we are done. The bottom line cost will be $50 to $100 per Iowan.

If only two classes per district use the network, the initial investment would represent $5,000 to $10,000 per student user. Therefore, it is imperative that other units of local government, hospitals, phone companies, cable television, and other private users be given access so capital costs can be recovered and user charges lowered. For example, if access charges run $350,000 for a hospital to access the network as reported, Iowa runs the risk of having an expensive high-tech network that sits idle.

Iowa Public Policy Education Project surveys show that Iowans have mixed emotions about the potential value of the fiber optics system. It is hard to evaluate something you don't understand or haven't seen in operation. Whether we like it or not, we now have a fiber optics system and the present challenge is to figure out how to use it and make it work, if possible.

There are some signs of hope. A PPEP Focus Group of diverse education leaders from across the state spent a day learning the hands-on uses of new teaching technologies, including fiber optics. The Focus Group survey indicated they ended the day with a much more supportive attitude toward completion of the fiber optics network. This suggests that attitudes of Iowans toward fiber optics may improve as more citizens learn how the system can be used. However, even Focus Group leaders agreed that small pilot demonstration programs should have been conducted before the state moved ahead with full construction.

If we are really serious about stimulating use and improving our state's competitiveness, perhaps we should consider the previous investment in fiber optics as sunken costs and allow free or low initial cost for accessing the system. This is similar to our policy on using the interstate highway system. It would generate experimentation and users who could eventually be charged fees to partially recover the initial investment.

The idea of pilot projects and demonstrations still makes sense. To fully utilize fiber optics and other teaching technologies, Iowa's schools, colleges, and universities will have to invest significant funds to produce quality educational programs and to train local teachers how to use and integrate these teaching technologies into local school programs. If a variety of pilot projects and demonstrations are conducted, local education officials could come to see what works and what doesn't before they make their own investments. If this "pump priming" is not done and if the fiber optics network is used only at a fraction of capacity, then history will refer to it as a boondoggle.

7. School Choice Has Been Oversold.

Nationally, school choice is related to tuition tax credits and vouchers. Under a voucher system, parents are given vouchers equal to the average annual costs of education per pupil. Parents can use the vouchers at the public or private school of their choice. In the case of tax credits, tuition costs are used to lower one's taxes by a like amount.

Two concerns are often raised about expanding school choice. One is separation of church and state. Some taxpayers have concerns about using public tax dollars to support religious educational activities. A second issue is that tax dollars might be used to create elite private schools. Since private schools are not required to accept all students, tax dollars could be siphoned to support "flight" from large urban public schools.

Recently Iowa has been willing to allow its public schools to provide private schools and home schools with increased access to public education resources and transportation services. But for the most part, the school choice issue in Iowa has a slightly different complexion from the national debate. Iowa was one of the first states to adopt open enrollment among public schools. In Iowa open enrollment was promoted as a way to give parents more choice and to improve the quality of education at the same time. In theory, if parents had the power to choose which public school in the state they wanted their kids to attend, then students would move from "lower quality" districts to "higher quality" districts. The theory sounds pretty good.

The market-oriented approach to public education supposedly rewards "good quality" districts and puts pressure to change on "poor quality" districts. Many lawmakers concluded that small schools should provide better quality education or consolidate.

The law prescribes that the total annual education cost per pupil goes with the student to the new district. This includes the student's state aid, local property tax support, and the cost of transportation for those who qualify. Districts with full classrooms may refuse to accept students.

Sending state aid dollars to a neighboring school district is one thing, but local citizens become upset when their property tax dollars go to support a neighboring district. Many consider this to be an excessive reward for schools that attract students. It also is an excessive penalty for the remaining students in districts that lose students. If the receiving district doesn't have to hire additional teachers but has empty classroom seats, the actual annual out-of-pocket costs for adding another student to fill an empty seat is about $250. However, the receiving district gains about $3,000 for adding the student and makes a profit of about $2,750 per student added, as long as more teachers aren't needed in the classrooms.

On the other hand, open enrollment adds significant stress to a small school district that may already be financially troubled. For every 10 students that leave for another district, one less teacher can be hired. This makes funding even more scarce at a time when officials would like to mount a school improvement program or an alternative education program. As a result, larger numbers of students remaining in the district end up with poorer quality education instead of improved programs.

In some cases, a stampede of students away from a school is created based on emotion. This emotion can overshadow school accountability indicators showing superior learning performance.

Apparently similar concerns also operate in Iowa's largest districts, including Des Moines and others. We shouldn't be surprised by this result. Most legislative ideas take years to pass; however, the Executive and Legislative leadership rammed open enrollment through and passed it within about six weeks from introduction in the General Assembly. Minnesota passed a similar law a year before Iowa. During Iowa's open enrollment debate, lawmakers heard from a Minnesota education official who said students were moving from the smallest districts up and from the largest districts down. That is what has happened in Iowa.

An Iowa Department of Education report on open enrollment for 1991-92 shows that Iowa's smallest districts experienced the largest outmigration as a percent of the student body. The largest districts in the state experienced the largest outmigration in terms of student numbers.

Why do the students move? Iowa's study concludes that school choice decisions were made for reasons of convenience, perceived education quality, school peer group, atmosphere conflicts, and sports. For 1991-92, 3,774 students requested open enrollment. This amounts to eight-tenths of one percent of Iowa's total student body. The study indicates that parents of students who open enroll show greater satisfaction. However, so far, no study provides evidence that statewide learning performance has improved.

If this is not the case, why should resident taxpayers and local schools be penalized with loss of state aid and property tax dollars to fund someone's choice and satisfaction? Iowa's commitment to each child is to provide equal access to a minimum standard quality of education. Those who desire to send their children to educational programs perceived to be superior are certainly entitled to a choice, but the public should not have to pay the extra costs. Why should students and taxpayers in districts left behind pay the costs?

What should be in the future? Parents should have school choice, but students, schools and taxpayers left behind should not be penalized. Transfer funding for open enrollment to receiving districts should be more in line with actual out-of-pocket expenses. Local property taxes should stay at home instead of supporting neighboring districts.

8. Student, Parent, Teacher and Community Involvement.

Real improvement in local education quality requires the involvement of parents, students, teachers and the community working together. Education experts suggest that parental involvement with children at an early age is very important to a child's success in school. However, a majority of today's children come from single parent homes and homes where both parents work. This leaves less time for parental involvement at home or at school. By the time a child reaches high school, parental participation in parent-teacher conferences drops off dramatically. We must create new ways to encourage and enable parents to stay involved with their kids and for kids to develop responsible attitudes.

Much of what happens now and later in life depends upon strong families and parenting skills at home. If parents allow their children to watch too much of the wrong kind of TV programs, it is no wonder they grow up to be couch potatoes lacking a sense of discipline or drive to take initiative in creating their own activities and solving their own problems. Many schools are looking at new innovative programs to help reinforce family values, parenting skills, and to recruit community or senior volunteers. These volunteers can provide role models and take interest in individual students in creating positive activities.

Communities and businesses are finding new ways to support education. Many innovative public-private partnerships are being developed. School officials and members of the business community are working together. In many cases, the schools are several years behind the business community in adopting new technologies and information. The new programs are designed to help make education programs more relevant for students, to give students an opportunity to examine new technologies, and to give students practical experience in the world of work and responsibility. At the same time, many business people are finding that if schools were run with the standards of many private sector corporations, we would have to add people and investment. Cooperative education programs often result in two way educational opportunities.

9. Will Iowa's School Transformation Be the Answer?

The Governor played an instrumental role in generating the present national education reform movement. In the late 1980s, he served as chair of the National Governors' Association effort that developed the first set of national education goals. In turn, this led to a national school transformation movement that is now being widely discussed in education circles.

School transformation is a word that means different things to different people. According to one dictionary definition, transformation means "to change the outward appearance." According to other definitions, "transformation" means total, complete, or fundamental change.

Similarly in Iowa, transformation has come to mean different things to different interests. To some interests, transformation means "site based management." This means shifting control over the educational process from the state and local school boards and administrators to teams of principals, teachers, and parents.

What one thinks about this form of school transformation depends in part on the present performance of his or her local school district. It is a mistake to presume that all Iowa schools are poorly managed. Many Iowa schools have delegated authority to teachers for years and have done their best to get parents more involved with teachers. However, good managers and good teachers are always looking for new ways of doing things better. Therefore, the transformation planning process may help them to make the best better.

To other interests, transformation means shifting the state school accreditation policy from standards based on inputs such as the pupil/teacher ratios and number of course units provided to standards based on output measures such as standardized competency performance tests.

Shifting from input to output standards for accreditation would seemingly breathe new life into some of the smaller school districts. Contrary to what many people believe, historically, half of the small rural school districts score above the largest school districts on standardized student performance tests. Therefore, small schools with high test performance may have the opportunity to waive traditional accreditation standards as long as they remain financially viable and provide a range of course offerings acceptable to local citizens. In addition, other larger schools may gain new information about the performance of their students. Therefore, transformation may help them to improve as well.

Still other interests say transformation means providing fiber optics and a computer for every child in Iowa. Many school districts have already provided computers for students to use. Other schools have used satellite course offerings from remote teaching stations for years.

Education research concludes that high quality remote teaching programs by satellite or fiber optics can be as effective as having a teacher in the classroom. However, the research also indicates that the economics of remote teaching only pays in certain cases. When a certain enrollment level is reached, it often becomes more cost-effective to hire a teacher in the classroom instead of paying the program access fee. Therefore, most remote teaching will likely be confined to advanced or specialized courses and for accessing information not locally available. In these cases, the transformation process may help schools discover cost-effective ways of using new teaching technologies in the classroom.

Finally, transformation means increased time for professional improvement, for planning creative teaching strategies, and access to funds for salary enhancement. Teachers have asked for more time to learn new teaching technologies, to develop creative teaching strategies, to consult with colleagues and to experiment with pilot programs. Other districts will beef up summer school programs, school enrichment programs, remedial programs, and/or gifted and talented programs. Therefore, transformation funding may help local boards and administrators continue to increase utilization of school property and sanction teacher time to examine ways of improving learning performance.

10. What Do Citizens Need for Accountability?

In the final analysis, school transformation sounds like a good thing. It has the potential to make Iowa's best in the nation education system a little bit better. But, will it really be as good as it sounds? And, how will we ever know whether it has done anything to improve educational opportunity and performance of our students? Or is this just another status quo initiative for throwing dollars at problems with no real accountability? How will we know which strategies did the trick and which ones didn't? How will we know which schools are making the grade and which ones aren't? How will we know whether we have gotten our money's worth?

The bottom line is that citizens and community leaders won't know unless someone is charged with the responsibility to keep score in an objective manner. And, then they must have the courage to provide politically unpopular information to the public, so that schools, boards of education, administrators and teachers can be held accountable. In recent history, Iowa's status quo leaders have not demonstrated a desire for this level of accountability or disclosure of school performance information to parents, taxpayers, and citizens.

In contrast, the Iowa Business and Education Roundtable report *World Class Schools* provided a range of indicators for each of their desired outcomes. Most of the indicators can be measured in an objective manner. However, it remains to be seen whether they will be used in any standardized fashion statewide.

During the past two years, Iowa's Department of Education has involved more than a hundred educators from across the state in a similar attempt to develop a second list of educational outcome goals. However, this second attempt failed and the effort was dropped in May 1993.

After reviewing earlier drafts of the Education Department's goals, I can see why some groups objected. Goals on diversity and environmentalism appeared to reflect a political agenda and had very little to do with academic performance measures. Similar citizenship goals were stated by the Business Education Roundtable, but in a less politically sensitive way. In public policy education we must recognize there is no one right solution. While parents and special interests are not entitled to their own set of facts on these issues, each is entitled to their own set of values. Therefore, such education goals must focus on presenting a balanced set of unbiased perspectives.

In dropping the statewide effort, it was suggested that local districts develop their own goals for educational outcomes. This is where the discussions of setting educational goals should have started in the first place. Setting outcome goals is a local school board responsibility. However, this does not mean that the state has no responsibility in the area of school accountability. It is still the state's responsibility to measure outcome indicators so local leaders and citizens can make district comparisons.

I have worked with several local citizen discussions on whether or not it made sense to consolidate schools with a neighboring district. Citizens in the audience were universally interested in district by district comparison of inputs, costs and student performance indicators. They felt this information was important in deciding which school plan would provide the most of the best for the least. They want to know how their school taxes, state aid and teacher salaries compare to neighboring districts and other districts in the state. They want to know how their pupil/teacher ratios and course offerings compare to the neighbors and others in the state. They want to know how their students perform on standardized achievement or competency tests compared to neighboring districts and others in the state and nation.

Some citizens may conclude that we can do too much testing. Therefore, we must be sure that we test only the appropriate skills and capacities regarding student learning. Yet, the tests should not be biased for or against a particular religion, race, or partisan political agenda. Citizens must be assured that students become responsible citizens who can think on their own.

Competency tests are not a replacement for personal student goals and local district performance goals. PPEP surveys of parents and school officials agree that individual student performance should be evaluated on individual progress indicators agreed to by teachers, parents, and students. However, school accountability is different from assessing individual student performance. If citizens and community leaders are going to judge accountability of their district, they need information on inputs, costs, and performance indicators to compare with neighboring districts and others across the state and nation.

An Iowa Public Policy Education Project survey shows that parents and citizens tend to agree that district by district comparisons of input costs and performance indicators should be available to the public. However, teachers and school officials tend to disagree and do not want such information made public.

A few years ago, Iowans were promised a Report Card on Iowa Schools. However, it was quickly discovered that district by district performance comparisons can create political fallout. By definition half of the state's school districts are below average. Since then, the Iowa Department of Education has been reluctant to release any information on performance indicators that can be used to make district by district comparisons.

It is a contradiction for Iowans to support school choice on one hand, but not provide parents and students with performance and accountability information to make school choices on the basis of quality. Regardless of whether the information is sensitive or not, Iowans have a right to know which school districts are doing the best job, so others can emulate them.

Iowans also have a right to know which districts are doing the poorest job, so that we can discover why and take actions to improve their results. We may find there are reasons unrelated to the education system that explain the poor indicators. If so, at least we know. Then future performances of the school districts can be judged relative to the base year indicators.

If Iowa is going to encourage wide scale experimentation and pilot projects in local districts, community leaders and citizens need more detailed performance evaluation indicators to know what is working and what isn't. Every business person knows that if one is serious about quality, one must evaluate the output and compare it with the competition. Otherwise, progress toward education quality may be two steps forward and two steps back.

The ultimate power and responsibility in a democracy rests with the people. It is the duty of citizens and community leaders to hold schools and political leaders accountable for the quality of education provided. Objective fact-based information on the performance of our public institutions is essential for citizen accountability. If such information is not available, citizens can only make accountability judgments based on what political leaders and vested interests tell them.

Education is a primary responsibility of state government. Therefore, it is a responsibility of Iowa's political leadership to assure statewide accountability. The political sensitivity of district accountability information can be lessened by publishing a range of indicators on inputs, costs, ratios, and performance. However, there may still be risks for status quo politicians, if the quality of education resulting from initiatives on school transformation, fiber optics, and school choice do not measure up to the political rhetoric citizens have been given.

The question is whether Iowa leaders will place greater priority on partisan political interests or will Iowa place greater priority on education accountability and full disclosure of the facts to parents, citizens and the taxpayers of Iowa.

Chapter 7. Iowans At The Crossroads.

1. The Right Leadership for the Times.

The previous chapters in this book have demonstrated that Iowans are truly at a crossroads. Average citizens and community leaders must seize the moment and decide whether to continue on with the status quo or to turn the corner toward new priorities and new opportunities.

The path of the status quo will look similar to what we have seen for the past decade with new wrinkles. We will see an economic base that will likely continue to erode and an aging population. We will see tax policies that are average among the 50 states. When these two factors are combined, we will see continued erosion of our jobs base and periodic reappearance of budget problems in future decades.

We must take calculated risks and test bold, but prudent, new ideas. All Iowans, rich and poor, have a stake in Iowa's future. Instead of cutting up a smaller and smaller pie, we must take dramatic action to expand Iowa's economic pie. Instead of striving for average economic policies, we must strive to be different and better.

Marketing campaigns will no longer do. We must put our money where our mouths are. All Iowa citizens must be encouraged to increase our savings and to invest in Iowa's future. That is how the Japanese did it. That is how the Germans did it. That is how Iowa can rebuild our jobs base and show the rest of this nation how it can be done.

But first, we must restore the integrity of Iowa's Constitution, which has been ignored for a decade. We must balance our budget using honest accounting and fiscal responsibility.

We must restore government by principle—not government by ruling elite and special interests. We must restore high principles and integrity in our government enterprises. All citizens, regardless of wealth, position, or philosophy must have confidence that our government will act with the highest standards of ethics and fair play for all citizen interests. This is called equal justice under the law and statesmanship over partisanship. Our highest leaders must respect these principles as well as the average citizens.

We all must roll up our sleeves and ask each citizen to do his or her part in repairing our health care system. Similarly, citizens must be prudent in transforming our education system, so that we keep Iowa first in the nation in education.

To do this, Iowans must depart from the status quo. We must insist on full disclosure of public information. If we do, more citizens will gain confidence in using their power and responsibility for holding political leaders and public institutions accountable for their actions and performance.

We must demand more from our gubernatorial and legislative candidates than TV commercial wars and debate over the finer points of political partisanship. Instead of cloudy visions and promises, we must insist that each candidate provide a practical plan for moving this state forward.

Each candidate should provide a blueprint for action on the issues that really matter to Iowa's future: rebuilding Iowa's jobs base, restoring fiscal integrity and government by principle, repairing our health care system, keeping Iowa education first in the nation, and others.

When Abraham Lincoln was faced with the prospect of civil war, he didn't worry about the opinion polls. He stood behind the principles upon which this nation was founded. When Harry Truman faced the aftermath of World War II, he didn't hesitate. He rebuilt the world's economic capacity.

Our Governors and Legislators must see past the moment. They must see past the special interests and partisan politics to what is in the best interest of Iowa citizens. They must be capable of building bridges and making the right decisions in a crisis. It is usually the crisis that shapes our future. They should set the standard of public behavior, demonstrate principles, and provide leadership by example. Only then will our children learn to respect the principles of citizen government and develop an ability to defend the principles from future abuses of power. That is the standard by which the Governors and Legislators of Iowa should be measured.

If the citizens of Iowa believe in the principle that leaders of a democracy should put the interests of the state and its citizens above the interests of the candidate's party, then the citizens themselves must be willing to demonstrate this principle by voting for the candidates who can deliver statesmanship, regardless of their party affiliation.

2. Can One Person Make a Difference?

Given the right timing, circumstances, and the right issues, one seemingly average person can make a difference in our political process and public policy. Mothers Against Drunk Drivers (MADD) became a national movement after one mother with a story to tell stepped forward to say enough was enough. The power of media to capture the public attention played an important role and so did the large numbers of other parents who were moved to join the effort. But, the idea and commitment to change public policy started with one person.

Normally, one person cannot expect that his or her idea will be taken as the best solution and implemented into law. Almost all of our public policy is a product of compromise among diverse citizen interests. Citizens and interest groups are affected differently by the same policy because they have different values and different circumstances in life.

Perhaps the greatest value of public discussion and debate in strengthening democracy has been demonstrated by the PPEP Focus Groups. Citizens with diverse interests tend to develop a greater appreciation for other points of view and become more tolerant as they learn why other people hold differing views. As people learn the views of others, their own views about what should be done often change.

In a democracy, we redraw the lines of compromise over time. We can and we do make changes in public policy and alter the performance of our government. Sometimes the change is slow. Other times the change can happen rather quickly. Each issue has different dynamics depending in part upon the importance of the issue and underlying support of the policymakers.

How many people does it take to change public policy in Iowa? In accordance with democratic principles, changes in the nature of the political processes as suggested in this book require large numbers of people and citizen interests saying the same thing. In fact, we would become concerned if a few special interests and power elite leaders could pass major changes if there was not broader support. Therefore, we as individuals should not expect our individual prescriptions for system change to be passed without the development of broad public support. The ideas must capture the imagination and support of the public.

On the other hand, we should not conclude that change requires the support of all citizens in the state. Far fewer people than you might think may be required to change policy.

In 1991, the Public Policy Education Project (PPEP) asked this question to state lawmakers in Iowa. On average, they said they receive about 10 constituent contacts on the average issue. In addition, lawmakers say they seek advice from three or four knowledgeable constituents on the average issue. If this is true, it takes 450 to 1,500 people statewide to influence Iowa public policy decisions on the average issue.

During the PPEP Focus Group discussions, one parent who became a lobbyist for home schooling suggested that 30 people committed to the same statewide goal could develop a strategy, write enough letters and make enough contacts to have an impact on state policy. If each of these 30 people found ten other people to write letters and make contacts at the appropriate time on the issue, they would have an impact. That is essentially how the home schooling bill passed in Iowa.

In conclusion, one person or a few people can make a difference. They make a difference by finding more people who are committed to the same concerns and by getting more people involved and capturing the attention of the media and general public. The process of restoring Iowa's democracy requires the same kind of effort.

Citizen by citizen, Iowans would need to move the "Restore Iowa's Democracy" agenda forward by expressing similar views publicly. Community by community, leaders would need to express similar views publicly. In the beginning, Iowa's media can help or hurt the process. But the bottom line is that enough people and interest groups must become convinced that the status quo is unacceptable and that greater citizen participation can make a difference in the performance of our government. If this happens, Iowa's democracy can and will be restored for this and future generations to come.

"Never doubt for a moment that a small group of thoughtful citizens working together and committed to a common goal can change the world. It is the only thing that ever has." Margaret Mead, American anthropologist.

SELECTED REFERENCES

Chapter 1. Rebuilding Iowa's Jobs Base and Economy.

Iowa Department of Employment Services. "Iowa Statewide Occupational Projections, 1992-2000." Jan. 1993.

Iowa Department of Economic Development. "A Five-Year Economic Development Plan, 1992 Update." Jan. 1992.

Pins, Kenneth. "Mixed Grade for Iowa's Economy." *Des Moines Register*, 6 May, 1993.

Fowler, Veronica and Holli Hartman. "Marshalltown Keeps Lennox Plant." *Des Moines Register*, 8 May, 1993.

KPMG Peat Marwick. "Report of the Study of Iowa Tax System." Dec. 1992.

Kasler, Dale. "Jet Factory Plan Stumbles." *Des Moines Register*, Apr. 1993.

"Challenging Trends: Indicators of Well-being for Iowa Children." Child and Family Policy Center, Des Moines, 1992.

"Family Economics Review." U.S. Department of Agriculture, 1993.

Goudy, Willis and Sandra C. Burke. "Iowa's Counties: Selected Population Trends, Vital Statistics, and Socioeconomic Data." ISU Census Services, 1992.

Immerman, Mark A. and Dan Otto. "Iowa Employment, Earnings, and Income, 1980-88." ISU Rural Data Project, Jun. 1991.

Iowa Senate. "Senate File 400, An Act Relating to Tax Exempt Municipal Bonds." Iowa General Assembly, 1993.

Iowa House of Representatives. "House File 196/Senate File 113. An Act Relating to a Property Tax Exemption for Machinery and Computer Equipment." Iowa General Assembly, 1993.

Iowa Senate. "Senate File 11. An Act Providing for the Establishment of Agricultural Enterprise Zones, etc." Iowa General Assembly, 1993.

Rosenfeld, Stuart, Philip Shapira and J. Trent Williams. *Smart Firms in Small Towns*. The Aspen Institute State Policy Program, 1992.

Perot, Ross. *United We Stand*. Hyperion NY, 1992.

"Invest or Die." *Fortune Magazine*, 22 Feb.1993.

Swenson, David, "A Study of Intergovernmental Revenue Impacts of the Taxpayers' Rights Amendment." Report to Iowa State Education Association, Iowa Association of School Boards, and School Administrators of Iowa, Dec. 1992.

Velie, Edward. "Review and Critique of Iowa School District Revenue Impacts of the Taxpayers' Rights Amendment." Iowa Association of School Boards, Jan. 1993.

Howard, Marcia A. "State Tax and Expenditure Limitations: There Is No Story." National Assn. of State Budget Officers, 1988.

Joyce, Philip G. and Daniel R. Mullins. "The Changing Fiscal Structure of State and Local Public Sector: The Impact of Tax and Expenditure Limitations." *Public Administration Review*, May 1991.

Snell, Ronald K. "State Tax and Expenditure Limitations." Outline of remarks to State Budget and Budgeting Practices Study Committee, National Conference of State Legislatures, Oct. 1991.

U.S. Congressional Budget Office. "Assessing the Decline in the National Saving Rate." Apr. 1993.

Waller, Robert James. *Iowa, Perspectives on Today and Tomorrow*. Iowa State University Press, 1991.

Chapter 2. Restoring Fiscal Responsibility.

"The Constitution of the State of Iowa." 1993 Iowa Code, General Assembly, 1992.

Patterson, Caleb, P. *The Constitutional Principles of Thomas Jefferson*. Peter Smith, 1967.

Fitzgerald, Michael, Treasurer of the State of Iowa. "Outstanding Obligations Report 1992." Jan. 1993.

State of Iowa. "$375,000,000, Tax and Revenue Anticipation Notes Series 1992," 8 July, 1992.

State of Iowa. "$96,030,000, Certificates of Participation, Series 1992A, Evidencing Ownership Interests in a Lease Purchase Agreement." 1 April, 1992.

Public Policy Education Project. "Solving Iowa's Budget Crisis: Iowa Public Opinion Survey on Iowa State Government Budget Issues." ISU Extension, Mar. 1992.

Public Policy Education Project. "Solving Iowa's Budget Crisis: Focus Group Report." ISU Extension, Jun. 1992.

Iowa Department of Revenue, "Iowa Property Tax Assessment Limitations." Unpublished information on assessment rollback adjustment and allowable growth, 1993.

Stanley et al vs Fitzgerald. "Appellants' Brief." Case 92-1234. The Supreme Court of Iowa.

Stanley et al vs Fitzgerald. "Appellee's Brief." Case 92-1234. The Supreme Court of Iowa.

Stanley et al vs Fitzgerald. "Appellants' Reply Brief." Case 92-1234. The Supreme Court of Iowa.

Stanley et al vs Fitzgerald. "Appendix." Case 92-1234. The Supreme Court of Iowa.

Osbun, Lee Ann and Steffen W. Schmidt. *Issues in Iowa Politics.* Iowa State University Press, 1990.

Chapter 3. Restoring Political Leadership.

Bowers, Claude G. *Jefferson and Hamilton: The Struggle for Democracy in America.* Houghton Mifflin Company, 1953.

Council of State Governments, *The Book of the States, 1992-93.* Table 2.1 The Governors, 1992.

National Council of State Legislatures. Unpublished Information on 1992 State Ballot Initiatives Regarding Term Limits, Dec. 1992.

Sage, Leland L. *A History of Iowa.* Iowa State University Press. 1990.

Black, Gordon S. "Perot Proposals Win Widespread Support" Gordon Black Corporation Poll: News Release, Rochester NY, 24 Mar. 1993.

Governor's Committee on Government Spending Reform. "Report on Recommendations of the Governor's Committee on Government Spending Reform." Dec. 1991.

Board of Regents. *Directory.* 1991.

"The Constitution of the United States." Commission on the Bicentennial of the United State Constitution, 1991.

Edelman, Mark A. "A Jeffersonian Award for Iowa Leadership." *The Des Moines Register,* Jul 28, 1992.

1993 Iowa Code. Chapter 13.2, Attorney General Duties.
1993 Iowa Code. Chapter 817, Special Powers of Police, Govenor and Attorney General.
1993 Iowa Code. Chapter 331.751, County Attorney.
1993 Iowa Code. Chapter 721, Offical Misconduct.
1993 Iowa Code. Chapter 722, Bribery and Corruption.

Chapter 4. Reinventing Local Government.

Iowa Department of Management. "County Government Administration Collaboration Plans." Unpublished spreadsheets of the Governor's Committee on Government Spending Reform, Feb. 1993.
"Senate File 399. An Act relating to the Charter Commission Process and Alternative Forms of Government, etc." Iowa General Assembly, 1993.
Edelman, Mark A. and James J. Knudsen. " A Classic Economies of Size Analysis on Average School Costs: An Iowa Case Study." *The North Central Journal of Agricultural Economics,* Jan. 1990.
Fox, William F. "Size Economies in Local Government Services: A Review." U.S. Department of Agriculture RDRR 22, Aug. 1980.
Henningson, Kelly. unpublished Iowa Sales Tax data, ISU Extension, Mar. 1993.
Otto, Daniel M. and Mark A. Edelman. "Innovation in Structural Change of Local Government." *American Journal of Agricultural Economics,* 1990.
Otto, Daniel M. "Issues in the Supply of Public Infrastructure." chp 3, *Local Infrastructure Investment in Rural America.* ed. Thomas G. Johnson, Brady J. Deaton and Eduardo Segarra. Westview Press, 1988.
DeBoer, Larry and Jeffery P. Mann. "City-County Consolidation for Indiana: An Outline of Issues." Purdue University, 1992.
Porter, Michael E. *Competitive Strategy.* Macmillan, 1980.
Swenson, David A. "Iowa Tax Facts for Financing State and Local Government." Iowa State University Extension, pm 1281, 1990.
Schmidt, Steffen W. "Future Roles and Accountability in Iowa Government." at The Iowa Budget: Progress and Prospects for the Future, ISU-CES conference, Des Moines, 8 Dec. 1992.

Harrigan, Kathryn R. *Strategies for Joint Ventures.* Lexington Books, 1985.

Chapter 5. Solving the Health Care Problem.

The Aging 2000 Committee Report. "Aging 2000: Directions for Elder Care in Rhode Island." Dec. 1991.

Blendon, Robert J., Robert Leitman, Ian Morrison and Karen Donelan. "Satisfaction with Health Systems in Ten Nations." *Health Affairs,* 1990.

Connet, Bill, Marilyn Musser, and Mark Wheeler. "Alternative Models for Financing and Delivering Health Care and Assuring Quality of Care." Iowa Health Reform Council, 26 May 1993.

Cordes, Sam M. "Rural Health Crisis." *Increasing Understanding of Public Issues and Policies,* Farm Foundation, 1991.

Edelman, Mark A. "Toward Public Judgement on Health Care Reform: A Community Based Public Choice Proposal." ISU Economics Dept Staff Paper 245, Nov. 1992.

Goodman, John C. and Gerald L. Musgrave. "Twenty Myths About National Health Insurance." National Center for Policy Analysis, Dallas, Tx., Dec. 1991.

Goodman, John C. and Gerald L. Musgrave. "Controlling Health Care Costs with Medical Savings Accounts." National Center for Policy Analysis, Dallas, Tx., Jan. 1992.

Hammond, David and Carol Volker. "A Closer Look at Health Care Policy: What is Iowa Doing?" ISU Extension HDFS-V-030a, Aug. 1992.

Iowa House of Representatives. "House File 2446." Iowa General Assembly, 1992.

Iowa Senate. "Senate File 2307." Iowa General Assembly, 1992.

Iowa Senate. "Senate File 380; An Act to Provide Greater Accessibility to Health Care and Health Insurance by Establishing Pilot Projects." Iowa General Assembly, 1993.

Iowa Leadership Consortium on Health Care. "Health Care Reform: A Proposal for Discussion by Iowans." Apr. 1992.

McDowell, George R. "The State of Rural Health Care System." *Increasing Understanding of Public Issues and Policies*, Farm Foundation, 1992.

National Center for Policy Analysis. "An Agenda for Solving America's Health Care Crisis." Task Force Report. Dallas, Tx., Jun. 1991.

National Issues Forums Institute. "The Health Care Crisis: Containing Costs, Expanding Coverage." 1992.

Oregon Health Services Commission. "Prioritization of Health Care Services: A Report to the Governor and the Legislature," 1991.

Public Policy Education Project. "Iowa Health Care Policy Preferences." Iowa State University Extension, 4 Apr. 1991.

Public Policy Education Project. "Iowa Health Care Focus Group Report." Iowa State University Extension, Oct. 1991.

U.S. Congressional Budget Office. "Rising Health Care Costs: Causes, Implications and Strategies." Apr. 1991.

U.S. Congressional Budget Office. "Selected Options for Expanding Health Insurance Coverage." Jul. 1991.

U.S. Congressional Budget Office. "Economic Implications of Rising Health Care Costs." Oct. 1992.

U.S. Congressional Budget Office. "Projections of National Health Care Expenditures." Oct. 1992.

Vincenzino, Joseph. "Trends in Medical Care Costs: A Look at the 1990s." Statistical Bulletin, Metropolitan Life Insurance Co., 1990.

Wellever, Anthony L. "Health Care Reform in West Virginia" Community Care Networks." draft. Rural Health Research Center, School of Public Health, University of Minnesota, May 1993.

Wolff, Michael, Peter Rutten, Alber F. Bayers III et. al. *Where We Stand*. Bantam Books, 1992.

Chapter 6. Keeping Iowa Number 1 in Education.

U.S. Department of Education. "America 2000: An Education Strategy." 1991.

Iowa Department of Education Strategic Planning Council. "A Blueprint for Excellence: Today's Vision — Tomorrow's Mission." 1991.

Iowa State Education Association. "Time for a Change: A Report to the People of Iowa from the Teachers of Iowa." 1991.

Iowa K-12 Education Reform Study Committee. "Blueprint for School Transformation." Legislative Service Bureau, Jan. 1993.

Iowa Department of Education. "Open Enrollment Report for the 1991-92 School Year." 1 Dec. 1992.

Iowa Business and Education Roundtable. "World Class Schools: The Iowa Initiative." 1991.

Johnson, Dale. "Examining Iowa's Fiber Optics Network Proposal." *Iowa Farm Bureau Spokesman*, 2 Nov. 1991.

Edelman, Mark A. "Is Fiber Optics the Road for Iowa To Take?" *The Des Moines Register*, 10 Mar. 1991.

Edelman, Mark A. and James J. Knudsen. "A Review of Research: Economies of Size and Impacts of Declining Enrollment on School Costs." Interim School Finance Study, ISU Econ Staff Paper 187, Jun. 1988.

Edelman, Mark A. and James J. Knudsen. "A Background Report: School Aid Goals, Parameters, Formulas and Impacts under Declining Enrollment." Interim School Finance Study, ISU Economics Staff Paper 188, Jun. 1988.

Edelman, Mark A. and James J. Knudsen. "A Review of State Programs: Adjustment Options for Declining Enrollments and Economies of Size." Interim School Finance Study, ISU Economics Staff Paper 189, Jun. 1988.

Edelman, Mark A. and James J. Knudsen. "An Analysis of Iowa School Spending Patterns and Size Characteristics." Interim School Finance Study, ISU Economics Staff Paper 194, Oct. 1988.

Edelman, Mark A. and James J. Knudsen. "An Analysis of Average and Marginal Costs of Iowa School Districts." Interim School Finance Study, ISU Economics Staff Paper 195, Oct. 1988.

Kniker, Eleanor L. and Mark A. Edelman. "Review of Literature on Remote Teaching Technologies and Teaching Effectiveness." ISU Economics Dept Staff Paper 221, Mar. 1991.

Public Policy Education Project. "Iowa Education Policy Preferences." Iowa State University Extension, Feb. 1992.

Bell, Julie D. "Distance Learning: New Technology and New Potential" State Legislative Report. National Conference of State Legislatures, Jul. 1991.

Brewton, Bobbretta Williams, "50 State Analysis of Education Reform Activities." Presented to K-12 Education Reform Study Committee, Iowa Legislature, 1992.

Chapter 7. Iowans at the Crossroads of the Future.

Public Policy Education Project. "Iowa Agenda Survey." Iowa State University Extension, Sept. 1991.

Public Policy Education Project. "Iowa Public Policy Education Project Final Project Report to the W.K. Kellogg Foundation." ISU Extension to Communities, Aug. 1992.